$\mathcal{P}$leasureland
$\mathcal{M}$emories

Pleasureland
Memories

A History of Southport's Amusement Park

STEPHEN COPNALL

SKELTER
PUBLISHING

First published in 2005 by
Skelter Publishing LLP
3 Connaught Road
St Albans
Herts
AL3 5RX

www.skelterpublishing.com

A catalogue record for this book is available from the British Library

ISBN 0-9544573-3-1

Designed and typeset in Great Britain by Paul Barrett Book Production, Cambridge.

With thanks to Justin Garvanovic and John Walton.

Printed by Thanet Press Ltd, Margate, Kent

Contents

*I dedicate this book to
my wife Maureen*

About the author

Stephen Copnall is a freelance teacher of Business German, Dutch and French. He has worked in Berlin, in West Germany, London, Liverpool and Manchester, teaching modern languages in schools and FE Colleges. Until recently, he was an associate lecturer at the University of Salford. He has lifelong family connections with Southport and an extensive knowledge of the town.

Acknowledgements

I hope that this book captures some of the flavour of times past and gives an accurate record of Pleasureland's development. I have trawled through council records, local newspapers, official holiday guides, Stephenson's and Southport Visiter guides, as well as drawing on my own notes and observations over the years. Unfortunately, apart from council minutes, no official records seem to have been kept, or if they were, they are no longer readily to be found. Pleasureland's ride owners and operators so often came and went, taking all documentation with them.

I was greatly encouraged by the late Geoffrey Thompson, former Managing Director of Blackpool Pleasure Beach, the present owners of Pleasureland, who replied enthusiastically to my letter in April 2004, as I first embarked on this project. My special thanks go to Blackpool historian and Pleasure Beach archivist Ted Lightbown and to his co-researcher Zena Burslam; without their help I could not have written this book. I am equally indebted to Robert Preedy, whose book 'Roller Coasters: Shake, Rattle and Roll' and advice on sources proved invaluable. My thanks go to Joanna Jones, curator of the Botanic Gardens Museum in Southport, who kindly reproduced many photos for research on the book, and to Andrew Farthing and his team in the Local History Unit at Southport's Central Library. They carried the heavy tomes of council minutes, guidebooks and newspaper articles from the Southport Visiter for me to study on numerous occasions.

I also owe a debt of gratitude to Joan Tarbuck who, in 1971, as Reference and Local History Librarian in the days of Southport Corporation, was incredibly helpful in looking up many references to Pleasureland in the archives of the time. These I kept for over thirty years to use in this publication.

I am also very grateful to Don Clark of the Lakeside Miniature Railway, who took the time to show me fascinating archive material and to Mr and Mrs Petrie, the proprietors of the now closed Southport Zoo next to Pleasureland, who outlined its history and the plans for the future of their life's work. My thanks, too, to the former directors of Peter Pan's Pool, Mr Ken Cam and Mr Douglas Maxwell, for answering my many questions.

Here I must mention Ray and Jean Jones of the delightful Model Railway Village, who gave me much useful information on the erstwhile 'Land of the Little People' behind the now defunct Lord Street Bus Station. Sefton Council is, and was, fortunate in having such attractions. Their owners have maintained them through the years, often – until recently – with little encouragement or support from the authorities. I trust that the Council's professed aim to re-establish Southport as a 'Classic Resort' will apply to every part of the seafront area and do justice to the heritage and the tremendous potential of the town. Certainly, the new Marine Drive, the spectacular new bridge over the Marine Lake, and the restoration of the Pier are a very promising start.

I hope that this book fills a gap in the many publications on and about this unique resort. I have tried to bring fresh material to light, but inevitably, some old ground will have been gone over again. What I hope comes across is a love of the town and a real wish that in the next five years Southport achieves the status that its history demands.

Almost everyone I have approached has been very helpful, particularly Mark Lee, Marketing Assistant at Pleasureland, who produced invaluable archive material and gave me a guided tour of the park. All the photographs reproduced in this book are courtesy of Blackpool Pleasure Beach Ltd, and originate from both the Pleasure Beach and Pleasureland archives, unless otherwise stated.

Finally, I must thank Nick Laister and Dave Page of Skelter Publishing, who were looking for someone to write a history of Pleasureland and who accepted my offer to do just that.

Stephen Copnall
Ilkley, July 2005

Introduction

Southport's seaside attractions are unique, in that they were all carefully laid out, in a vast municipally-planned marine park, in line with the town's reputation as a 'Seaside Garden City'. There was no haphazard development, although some post-war buildings are unworthy of the original aims of the Victorians and Edwardians. Inevitably, through the years, mistakes have been made, often due to an acceptance of short-term solutions. Nevertheless the overall impression a visitor gains is one of pleasant coherence against a background of beautiful western maritime skies and unforgettable sunsets.

From the age of seven, I was fortunate enough to be able to spend the wartime and post-war summer holidays in Southport, where my maternal grandparents and other relatives had lived since 1924. They would take me to Peter Pan's Pool and, when it re-opened, to Pleasureland. As I grew into my teens, I would go as often as I could to 'the fair', as it was then called, to sample every ride as far as pocket money would allow.

Many Sandgrounder families will, I suspect, have similar memories. Half a crown in the 1940s and 50s went quite a long way. The Cyclone cost a shilling, and was therefore the most expensive and exciting ride. The other rides were sixpence and many offered half price admission to children in those days. Pablo's and Creamland Ices were threepence and sixpence; the pre-war 'Stop-me-and-buy-one' Wall's ice cream carts had disappeared. Before the war and before my time, the Scenic Railway cost threepence and no ride was more than sixpence. What useful coins the threepenny bit and sixpence were!

In this special place there was an ever present breeze, the smell of sand and sea, and the bright colours of the freshly painted rides; a haven of fun and excitement in an otherwise drab world. Pleasureland still has that magic today, in the changed circumstances of the 21st century. It is still an amusement park loved by young and old.

ONE

❧

A tour of Pleasureland

I have an appointment with Pleasureland Marketing Assistant Mark Lee on Friday 30 April 2004. Mark will take me around Pleasureland as it is being prepared for the May Day Bank Holiday. The transformation wrought by Geoffrey Thompson and his management team since Blackpool Pleasure Beach gained complete control is truly amazing. Everywhere there is evidence of landscaping, careful renovation and imaginative use of space. Indeed, it is quite obvious that the only way now to expand is onto the adjacent grounds of the Zoo on the north side of the park which, thanks to Mr Thompson's vision, has been recently acquired for Pleasureland. A major new ride is promised there for 2006, as the animals are only gradually being rehoused, some in other zoos, some in a new home in North Yorkshire – a process which takes time.

The new Pleasureland entrance building under construction in January 2004.

(Photo: Nick Laister)

On South Road, leaving the Casablanca Restaurant and Entertainment Centre, we pass on our left the recently renovated and extended Funhouse and the dramatic icon of 1999, 'The Traumatizer', a suspended looping coaster, the largest in Britain when it was built. Mark explains that the former River Caves, which is the oldest ride in Pleasureland, having been relocated in 1922 to its present position when these grounds first opened, is now completely rebuilt and renamed. The scenic waterway will carry the boats through the Lost Dinosaurs of the Sahara.

Opposite is the Waterboggan, a twin slide acquired in the 1994 season following the much-lamented closure of Southport Sea Bathing Lake. Also facing the River Caves site is the 'wild mouse' type wooden roller coaster which was brought from Morecambe's Frontierland Theme Park, completely renovated and rebuilt as 'King Solomon's Mines' in 2000.

The twists and turns of the Traumatizer (2002).
(Photo: Nick Laister)

An aerial view from the top of the Traumatizer looking north, a year before the arrival of the Lucozade Space Shot. The 'King Solomon's Mines' wooden wild mouse coaster can be seen in the centre of the photograph.

'Abdullah's Dilemma', on the site of the pre-war House of Nonsense, is also a popular attraction in its new guise. In this corner of Pleasureland the Helters Company, in which Blackpool Pleasure Beach had shares, operated many different rides.

We take a right turn and walk down North Road in the shadow of the 1937 Cyclone wooden roller coaster, which replaced the veteran Helters Figure Eight coaster. Mark tells me that the way underneath the Cyclone to the Go-Kart Track has been temporarily closed to allow development to take place on the site of the Zoo. Adjacent to the Cyclone once stood the Ghost Train, converted from the Helter Skelter Lighthouse in 1931. It operated on that location until 1997, with the exception of the period 1941 to 1944 when it was requisitioned for the War effort. In 1998 its features were moved into the former Journey into Space, situated and built around the last lap of the Cyclone to form a new dark ride.

As we approach the Cyclone station entrance, Mark explains that the trains running on it are from the 'Grand National', a twin-track wooden roller coaster at Blackpool Pleasure Beach. The Cyclone became famous for having a backward-facing car, but this disappeared when the original cars were replaced. Now, for safety reasons, only two trains – instead of the former three – can operate simultaneously at peak periods.

On the right hand side of North Road are gravity rides designed for 'teens and twenties', such as the 'Tidal Wave', which is like a giant swing boat, and the new 2004 'Sandstorm', which rotates standing passengers at terrifying speeds. Here, from the immediate post-war period until the mid-1950s had been the Dodgems, the Cake Walk, a mini-coaster and the Octopus.

In the early 1980s a new way through under the Cyclone was created giving access to the Slippery Slopes Slide Park, the new Go-Kart track and other attractions of the area named Sportsland.
(Photo: Stephen Copnall)

The new Ghost Train opened in 1998 in the former 'Journey into Space' building. It featured spinning cars, and re-used many of the effects from the original Ghost Train, which closed in 1997. (Photo: Nick Laister)

A chained dinosaur steps across the River Caves track. This picture was taken just before work started on the upgrade of the River Caves into its new guise as the Lost Dinosaurs of the Sahara.

(Photo: Nick Laister)

The Octopus gave way in 1956 to the Hurricane Jets, a more popular ride which operated for decades on a strategic site across from the Cyclone and the Noah's Ark.

Before the war and the 1978 post-war extension of Southport Zoo, an important entrance from Princes Park gave north-south access to the southern side of Pleasureland, now a coach and car park. On this southern site were the two roller coasters of wooden construction, the Scenic Railway and the Mountain Caterpillar Railway. Tragically, these two rides were allowed to disappear during the requisition period and were only replaced properly in real terms when Geoffrey Thompson built the Traumatizer on a parallel site in 1999.

Today, around and within Pleasureland are attractive flowerbeds, plants, bushes, new paving and lighting. The old exterior walls, erected originally as part of the Town Council's attempt to renovate the grounds in 1949/50, are now being replaced by attractive undulating grassy banks and stone screens to give the environs the look of an inviting oasis on Southport sands.

Continuing our tour from the Cyclone onwards, we take a look at the extended children's Desert Rescue Ride and near it the Pleasureland Show Pavilion and Mistral Flying Machine. As we proceed, I notice that almost all the former stalls and sideshows have disappeared along North Road to be replaced by attractive booths, cafes and shops selling the paraphernalia of the seaside. 'The

An early morning view in May 2000. The Mistral Flying Machine and, left, the Wild Mouse. On the far right the Tidal Wave awaits the arrival of its mainly teenage clients. (Photo: Nick Laister)

Wild Cat', now located by the former entrance to the Zoo, and the aerial cableway known as the 'Skyride' are being tested for Saturday's opening. I see several cars running empty up and down the coaster's Pinfari track, imported from Italy in 1978, after the Noah's Ark was destroyed in a disastrous fire. It is one of two Pinfari coasters at Pleasureland, which can be moved to different sites within the park.

As we turn right again at the end of North Road, towering above us is the Lucozade Space Shot, opened by Neil and Christine Hamilton in 2002. This, the Cyclone and the Traumatizer are landmarks which can be seen from every point along the new Marine Drive. Indeed, the higher sea wall with its attractive promenade along the tide line to the rebuilt Southport Pier has given Pleasureland a location central to the new and ongoing development of Ocean Plaza.

We now return southwards to the new entrance building, opened in 2004, where ticket sales and admission numbers can be monitored through the turnstiles. Visitor numbers have been well over two million in recent seasons. On our right is the children's ride area with the Bowl Slide, Haunted Inn and the Caterpillar, which date from the time of the council's post-war reconstruction and retrenchment in 1949/50. There are many more attractions here for the age group which, from 1930 to 1970, were catered for at Peter Pan's Pool and Playground on the other side of Southport Pier by the Marine Drive Station of the Lakeside Miniature Railway.

As we near the end of our tour, Mark points out the Bingo and Amusement Arcade which runs the full length of the eastern side of the park up to the new entrance building. Catering in the vast Casablanca complex at the southern corner of Pleasureland and in all the other outlets is quality controlled by Blackpool Pleasure Beach and has resulted in a much higher and consistent standard of food and drink.

As I leave the park, I am deeply impressed by the metamorphosis which, thanks to Geoffrey Thompson's vision, has turned Pleasureland into one of Britain's leading seaside amusement parks. Now in a location which includes a hotel, a multi-screen cinema, a bowling alley and a shopping complex, plans are advanced for an 'aquadome' waterpark and another hotel. The Pleasureland of today is better than ever.

The Space Shot became a major landmark on the Southport skyline from 2002.
(Photo: Nick Laister)

A light-hearted touch. Geoffrey Thompson was to add 'National Historical Markers' to some of the older rides in Pleasureland. A Helter Skelter has been on this site since 1950 and was adapted into a Bowl Slide as shown on the plaque.
(Photo: Nick Laister)

A 1999 view of the Caterpillar which has continued to be a popular ride since it first arrived in Pleasureland in 1949.
(Photo: Peter Owen Creative Photography, Lytham St Annes)

Two

~

Southport's Origins

Lord Street in its Edwardian heyday circa 1909. The shops, with continuous verandas, stretch almost without interruption the full length of the boulevard.

(Photo: Nick Laister Collection)

The Lancashire coast from the Fylde to the Wirral Peninsula contains one of the largest and longest stretches of dunes and gently shelving firm sandy beaches in Britain. Where it has not yet been built upon, it could be compared with the unspoilt stretches of Jutland or the coastal strip of North and South Holland. The river estuaries of the Mersey and the Ribble punctuate these Lancashire shores, which enjoy a mild and pleasant climate, unknown to those who live elsewhere.

In the second half of the Eighteenth Century, sea bathing was becoming fashionable all over England. West Lancashire was largely isolated, sparsely inhabited and undeveloped. A beach two miles to the south west of Churchtown, a hamlet which goes back to the Twelfth Century, was gaining a reputation as an ideal place from which to bathe. An innkeeper from Churchtown, William Sutton, had erected a makeshift wooden shelter for bathers to rest at this spot on the coast which bore the name South Hawes. People were taken by cart or coach to bathe both from North Meols, the district in which Churchtown lay, and also from the canal bridge at Scarisbrick.

Several versions of the origins of Southport exist, but the general consensus is that William Sutton built a permanent structure in 1798, the materials for which were brought by boat from Liverpool to 'South Port', a corruption of the name South Hawes and this in turn was soon written and spoken as one word, Southport. As the popularity of the location soon increased, a start was made in 1835 on the construction of today's Promenade, between Nevill Street and Coronation Walk. A few years later, it was extended northwards to Seabank Road and until 1858 a charge of one penny was levied from those who wished to walk upon it.

Digging deep

The sea, as yet unaffected by the digging of a deep sea channel to Preston Docks, which took place between 1884 and 1888, was a force to be reckoned with at high tide. Bathing machines proliferated and other traditional pursuits of the seaside began to make their mark. Lord Street, originally named 'Lord's Street', lay along a valley between the sand hills and developed as the well-to-do middle classes, from the industrial areas of Lancashire to the south and east, erected marine villas and also boarding houses to accommodate visitors. The width of the street itself was 80 feet. The houses had long gardens stretching to the carriageway and survived on one side until the Twentieth Century, but on the north western side were gradually converted into shops, until by 1890 that aspect of Lord Street very much resembled what we know today.

Sea bathing was clean and safe; no pebbles or stones lurked to bruise the feet. The gentle, highly tidal salt waters and pure sea air were deemed beneficial to health. The shrimpers and cocklers, whose craft goes back centuries, found new markets for their produce, as visitors to the town grew in number, but increasingly turned their hand to other pursuits connected with the holiday trade.

Southport had become sufficiently important to be linked by railway in 1848 to Liverpool, in 1853 to Wigan, and by 1855 to Manchester, giving direct access to the two major centres of population in Lancashire. By 1861, the town – still a separate and distinct entity from its

Cocklers and shrimpers have always been a part of Southport's working traditions on the vast expanse of sands.
(Photo: Nick Laister Collection)

immediate neighbour Birkdale – had a population of 10,097 inhabitants. The Pier, built in 1860, stretched 1,200 yards out to sea. It was extended to a length of 1,460 yards by 1868 and today is second only in length to Southend Pier in Essex. The pier in Southport was needed to reach the deep channel, called the 'Bog Hole', which was used by steamers and other craft from Liverpool and Preston.

Sand yachting was another popular pastime on the firm stretches of beach until the construction of the North Marine Lake in 1891. The North Marine Lake joined the existing southern lake, which dated from 1887. Along the Promenade, gardens developed on the accumulations of sand and dunes as the tide line receded. It was here, at the southern end of the newly created Marine Lake and beyond the line of gardens, that the area known as the 'Fairground' developed on the foreshore.

In 1867, Southport was constituted as a municipal borough. By 1874, a Pavilion and Winter Gardens had opened at the southern end of the Promenade, preceded in 1873 by the opening of the first horse tram route from Churchtown via Roe Lane and Lord Street to Birkdale. Other extensions followed in 1880. In 1882, a railway line was built between Southport and Preston and another connection, from Lord Street Station to Liverpool, through the sand dunes via Ainsdale, was opened in 1884.

Wealth holds sway

Partly because much of the foreshore was in municipal hands, and the town proper under the control of large landowners, Southport developed along well planned lines with tree lined streets, detached or semi-detached villas and generously appointed public buildings. The same conditions applied to Birkdale which, to all intents and purposes, was indistinguishable from its more powerful neighbour. Wealthy residents, who inhabited the areas nearest the shore, very much held sway during these decades in deciding how the town should develop. A powerful religious lobby ensured that Sunday was strictly observed. Lord Street became an elegant boulevard; anything to do with the cheaper end of the market was kept firmly away from that street. It was at this period in the town's development that large hotels and hydropathic institutes, such as the vast Palace Hotel by Birkdale Beach, in 1866, and Smedley's Hydro further inland, in 1877, began to appear.

By 1900, moves were afoot to unite the two towns; the tram system was electrified throughout and county borough status was granted to Southport in 1905. In 1912, Birkdale, along with the southern extremity of Ainsdale, were amalgamated into one unit of administration, bringing the population of the newly enlarged town of Southport to over 50,000. The number of inhabitants had reached 78,925 by the census of 1931. Today, Southport, within the much larger Merseyside borough of Sefton, has a population of 90,000 in its own right, defying all the trends of falling numbers evidenced in some parts of the North West.

As the industrial areas of Lancashire and West Yorkshire developed, so the resorts of Blackpool and Southport attracted its vast population as holidaymakers, and to a lesser extent as residents, so good were the railway connections of the time. Today it is easy to fail to recognise how advanced these towns were, a point not lost on entrepreneurs who were capable of looking beyond London to the powerhouses of the north, where the speed of development, along with an American 'get-up-and-go' attitude, were quite breathtaking. When the catastrophe of the 1914–18 Great War dealt its crippling blow, things thereafter were, as the saying goes, never the same.

THREE

Rising from the sands

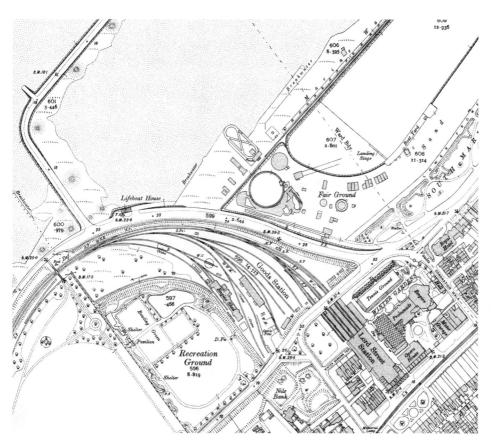

A 1909 plan of the fairground showing the Figure Eight, the Water Chute and part of the vast Lagoon area within the Marine Drive. The Cheshire Lines Railway to Lord Street Station and the Winter Gardens complex, put to various uses over the years, would largely disappear by the mid-1950s.

At the turn of the Twentieth Century, Southport had already become one of the most important holiday resorts in the country. The Town's main infrastructure that can be seen today was already largely in place. Now well established, the gardens in front of the Promenade had been laid out as far as the landward side of the lake. Beyond, towards the sea, stretched an area of grassland known as the Lagoon. On three sides of a square, so to speak, the Marine Drive – completed in 1895 – marked out the many acres of the foreshore, from the Pier to the Esplanade, ripe for further development.

The Lagoon was subject to flooding when very high tides occurred. These could sweep across the Marine Drive – then much lower than today – onto the sandy wetlands on the other side. North of the Pier, the sand reached in an uninterrupted expanse to the rim of the Marine Lake itself. Given the right tidal conditions, seawater could and did pour into the lake.

Landowners had sold to the council their rights to the Foreshore on condition that it would be used for public recreational amenities and that it remained firmly under corpora-

A stall selling Southport Rock and an impromptu show on the sands underscore the random nature of attractions on the Foreshore before the opening of White City in 1911.
(Photo: Sefton Libraries Local History Unit, Southport)

An early 1900s view of the Foreshore Fairground, looking towards the Promenade and, far right, the Southport Winter Gardens. Note the simple water channel roundabout device known as the Ocean Wave, in the centre foreground. This ride was transferred to the 1922 Pleasureland, where it continued to operate for several years.
(Photo: Sefton Libraries Local History Unit, Southport)

tion control. On the sands, from 1870 onwards, there had gathered a collection of shies, stalls and simple rides. This haphazard assembly was the beginning of Pleasureland Amusement Park, although it would not be called 'Pleasureland' for many years.

Ramshackle order

Everything remained ramshackle until the arrival of larger amusement devices dictated the need for some sort of order to be imposed on what was now known as the 'Fairground'. By 1895, the two halves of the Marine Lake were joined and the Marine Drive constructed. This involved the removal of all of the fairground paraphernalia under the pier by Nevill Street to the south end of the lake. Local shrimpers and fishermen had worked on the fairground on their own initiative but, by 1895, a Switchback Railway – the forerunner to today's roller coasters – was open to the public. The ride was identical to those operating in other resorts.

One of the other early rides at Southport was the 1895 Aerial Flight, which traversed the southern end of Southport's Marine Lake by means of gondola style boats, suspended on moving wires above the water. These were accessed by climbing flights of stairs to an elevated platform from the sands below. On descending at the other end of the ride, an area for paddling and buckets and spades, known as the Children's Paradise, could be reached. Refreshment bars, ice cream, ginger beer, lemonade, tea and coffee stalls were prominent amongst the photo studios, the Punch and Judy show, gipsy fortune tellers, coconut shies and simple amusement devices. A little further northwards, the Pier Pavilion featured twice daily entertainment, provided at 3.30 and 7.30 by the Pierrots. These were concert party entertainers with pointed hats, white faces and harlequin-style uniforms, popular at the time and remaining so as end-of-the-pier entertainment until the 1950s.

The fair and the crowds who visited it were now sufficient to come to the attention of a man by the name of WG Bean, a Londoner who had spent many years in America seeking his fortune. Whilst in America, he had become involved in the manufacture of rides for the

View of the Aerial Flight looking towards the Pier Pavilion. The 1895 attraction was removed from the sands in 1911 as residents objected to what they considered to be an eyesore. (Photo: Botanic Gardens Museum, Southport)

country's embryonic amusement park industry. Visits to developing parks such as New York's Coney Island had inspired him to try ideas on the much less-developed British amusement industry. Bean owned the sole UK rights to the newly developed American ride, the 'Hotchkiss Bicycle Railway', a contraption on which riders pedalled their way along an elevated track. Bean was already operating Bicycle Railways at Great Yarmouth and Brighton and had decided to try his luck at the increasingly popular Southport.

Southport was very popular in the early decades of the Twentieth Century, but Blackpool overtook it rapidly both in size and number of visitors. Residents and ratepayers exerted a greater influence on how Southport developed, resulting in the removal of the Aerial Flight by 1911 and, until 1954, the closure of most attractions on Sundays.

(Photo: Sefton Libraries Local History Unit, Southport)

One of the first rides to come to Southport sands, the Switchback, was the forerunner of the roller coasters we know today. In the foreground is the Bicycle Railway.

**The River
Caves in the
opening year
of 1908 with
a rear view
of the 1905
Helter Skelter
Lighthouse.**
(Photo: Botanic
Gardens Museum,
Southport)

Only a year later, in 1896, Bean would also take his Bicycle Railway to Blackpool, a town in which he would settle. The Bicycle Railway was Bean's first ride in Blackpool, but he would considerably develop his attractions in the town, becoming the founding father of the famous Pleasure Beach amusement park. Bean was the father of Doris Thompson and grandfather of Geoffrey Thompson who from 1976 until 2004 jointly directed the affairs of the huge enterprise in Blackpool, as Chairman and Managing Director respectively, and would both play massive roles in the development of Pleasureland.

As with so many things, the United States was in the lead in the development of amusement parks. Many new and exciting rides had their origins in the burgeoning pleasure resorts of New York's Coney Island, Atlantic City and the White City of 1893 in Chicago. The River Caves (a journey by boat through tunnels and caves with tableau representing exotic parts of the world) the Switchback and Scenic Railways (both forerunners of today's roller coasters) as well as other devices came from the United States and were brought to Blackpool in the first instance (in 1905, 1891 and 1906 respectively), but also to Southport.

Out of the equation?

By the 1890s, Blackpool's growth was beginning to outstrip that of Southport and it was becoming a focal point for the establishment of spectacular amusement devices and seaside leisure activity. In 1894 the town had its own version of the Eiffel Tower which formed the centrepiece of a vast covered entertainment complex right on the seafront. This was followed in 1896 by the erection of a Big Wheel over 200 feet high. A replica of this survives in full working order at the Viennese amusement park, known as the Prater. Both wheels were manufactured in Blackpool, highlighting the dynamic engineering skills of the era. As the age of mass entertainment dawned, Southport could not be left out of the equation.

Although those with political power and influence wanted to keep the town as genteel as possible, there was a conflict of interest with those catering for the demands of the holiday trade. It was impossible to deter trippers flocking in ever-greater numbers, not only to Blackpool, but also to Southport, where the fairground was a major attraction. Workers in the cotton industry were, by the standards of the day, in regular employment, earning above-average wages and could now enjoy several days of unpaid holiday per year as well as official bank holidays. By 1911, however, the Aerial Flight had been dismantled thanks to the protests of residents on the Promenade who forced its closure. They objected to the fact that this "ugly contraption" marred their sea views. Those responsible for the tasteful development of the foreshore wanted the rides moved to the south eastern corner of the Marine Lake, where indeed development proceeded apace.

In 1903, a Water Chute was opened by the Southport Boating Company, which held the main concession on the lake. The Company chose the southern extremity on which to build it. From a high platform, passengers entered a flat-bottomed boat which then descended on rails to splash at the end of the chute into the Marine Lake. It was then ferried to the water's edge, to deposit its human cargo, before travelling back up to the elevated stage, drawn by a mechanical chain. This was the first such device in any of Britain's coastal towns, ahead even

The Promenade looking south in the early 1900s, before the widening of the carriageway. Note the position of the 1895 Aerial Flight, to which so many residents objected.
(Photo: Sefton Libraries Local History Unit, Southport)

Another view of the Aerial Flight with a gondola car, suspended on cables, moving above the sands and Marine Lake.
(Photo: Nick Laister Collection)

The Water Chute before its removal from the Marine Lake to Pleasureland.
(Photo: Nick Laister Collection)

The Water Chute always drew tremendous crowds of onlookers and remained a premier attraction until it was dismantled and sold for scrap at the end of the 1940 season, when Pleasureland closed for five long years during the War.
(Photo: Sefton Libraries Local History Unit, Southport)

of a similar one in Blackpool, which opened in 1907. Until 1920, Southport was actually a much larger town than its rapidly expanding neighbour and in the very early years of the Twentieth Century, its amusement park was certainly more advanced. Indeed, very similar or identical rides appeared in both fairgrounds as the owners of these rides, such as Helters and WG Bean's Hotchkiss Patents, had a foot in both camps.

In 1904, there was a further Blackpool connection. Another manufacturer of devices, Sir Hiram Maxim, the inventor of the machine gun, erected a 'Captive Flying Machine' ride at Southport a few weeks after he had opened a similar one in Blackpool, a ride which is still operating at Blackpool Pleasure Beach. Maxim was an American engineer who had always been interested in flight. His Flying Machine ride at Southport consisted of ten boat-like cars suspended chair-o-plane style above a large circular landing stage. As the 'planes' began to revolve, they swung out over the Marine Lake below, greatly adding to the thrill. The ride was very popular.

Southport Fairground, 1904. The men look cheerful having accomplished their task of building Sir Hiram Maxim's Captive Flying Machine.

A fascinating photo of the many sideshows and stalls on the Foreshore Fairground. On the left is the 1895 Switchback Railway, forerunner to today's wooden roller coasters. Beyond the Water Chute is a collection of swingboats which were operated by pulling on ropes.

(Photo: Nick Laister Collection)

To the lighthouse!

Another ride common to both Southport and Blackpool was the Helter Skelter Lighthouse, built in 1905. This identical twin to the one at the Pleasure Beach was owned by Helters. The Helters organisation was partly owned by Pleasure Beach management who, from the outset, had shares in the company. By 1908, the first of a number of major exhibitions began at the White City, then Earl's Court in West London, culminating in the 1924 Empire Exhibition at Wembley. These events were complemented by an amusement park featuring the latest devices, which influenced developments elsewhere, particularly at coastal locations such as Southport and Blackpool. The name White City became synonymous with a place of amusement of a mainly mechanical nature – hence the same name being adopted for a short time in Southport, and on a more permanent basis in Manchester, where the White City amusement park in Stretford was a rival to Belle Vue.

One of the many comic seaside postcards on sale in 1905.
(Photo: Sefton Libraries Local History Unit, Southport)

A roundabout on the Foreshore circa 1905.
(Photo: Sefton Libraries Local History Unit, Southport)

An excellent view circa 1906 of the Helter Skelter Lighthouse with the stairs leading to and from the Bicycle Railway. (Photo: Sefton Libraries Local History Unit, Southport)

Below: This picture from 1908 shows the Figure Eight. The entire structure was moved to Pleasureland in 1922, with the entrance moved to the side.

(Photo: Sefton Libraries Local History Unit, Southport)

Taken in 1908, the Figure Eight Toboggan Railway lasted until the end of the 1936 season. Here it stands on the edge of the Lagoon next to Hiram Maxim's Captive Flying Machine.

In 1908 a Figure Eight Toboggan Railway was built on the grassland on the seaward side of the Marine Lake and a River Caves, an idea from America and already in Blackpool, was opened in the fairground itself. The River Caves, described as "a scenic waterway in tunnels" featured various tableaux and made ingenious use of boats which were propelled in a strong current, powered by a motor driven paddle wheel. The Figure Eight, patented in America but seemingly having various designers in Britain, was the first roller coaster with a continuous circuit, avoiding the need on the Switchback Railway to turn the cars around manually at the

The Fairground before the name of White City became generally accepted. From left to right: the curved roof of the House of Nonsense, the River Caves, the top of the Helter Skelter and the Water Chute. Through the supports of the Water Chute one can see the Pier stretching out to the landing stage where steamers from such exotic places as Llandudno, Lytham and Blackpool called until the silting of the channel after 1923.

(Photo: Nick Laister Collection)

White City, Southport, in 1911. From left to right, Hiram Maxim's Captive Flying Machine and Llewelyn's miniature railway. A steam train is ready to depart from White City Station on its way to the Pier Station.

A 1913 view of White City with, left to right, the Helter Skelter lighthouse, the House of Nonsense behind the Water chute, the Captive Flying Machine and the Figure Eight.
(Photo: Nick Laister Collection)

The beach and part of the Foreshore Fairground looking along the edge of the Promenade Gardens to the entrance of the Aerial Flight.
(Photo: Sefton Libraries Local History Unit, Southport)

end of the straight track. Figure Eights – the name was even adopted in Germany as the 'Achterbahn' – appeared in amusement parks all over the country and soon ousted the pioneer Switchback as the most common roller coaster ride.

When the Aerial Flight disappeared, there was further impetus for change. In May 1911, Llewellyn's Miniature Railway opened and, at the same time, the name of the amusement park was changed to 'White City', witnessed by the name of Llewellyn's station, which took passengers on steam trains along the seaward side of the Marine Lake to the Pier. This was several hundred yards away from the Pier Entrance and Pavilion, but very handy for the Children's Seashore Playground on the sandy shore of the Marine Lake. In the same year a House of Nonsense, almost identical to one in Blackpool and a forerunner to today's Fun House, was built at White City. This edifice contained numerous devices such as moving staircases, false walls and floors, spinning turntables, a hall of mirrors and a maze. For a one admission ticket visitors could partake of everything on offer. Another attraction, again replicated in Blackpool Pleasure Beach, was the appearance of the Joy Wheel. This was a vast revolving disc with a raised portion on which participants sat. As the device began to spin, it forced the revellers to tumble off the edge in a variety of rather undignified poses, causing general mirth and hilarity amongst the many onlookers.

In October 1912, at the close of the season, the original part of White City disappeared to allow work on widening the Promenade to begin. The rides which had joined the fair since the start of the decade were not affected and, by 1913, the Municipality of Southport, which was the driving force behind change and improvement (rather than private enterprise, which was the case in nearby Blackpool), had laid out the King's Gardens at the south end of the lake.

A council landfill scheme was planned for the Lagoon and, by 1914, an open air seawater bathing lake had been constructed on the north western corner of the Marine Drive. This site would later be occupied from 1930 by Peter Pan's Pool and Playground and finally in the 1970s and 1980s by Happiland, an amusement park exclusively designed for children.

Full of beans at White City

With the change of name to White City and its relocation away from the Promenade, the area gained a respectability it had not enjoyed before. The amusement park was following in the footsteps of WG Bean's Pleasure Beach at Blackpool. Bean disliked the term 'fairground' and, from 1905, was using the name of 'Pleasure Beach' to describe his Blackpool enterprise. The official holiday guides were already lauding the improvements thus far achieved. In the 1913 edition of the excellent Stephenson's Guide, produced with loving care on the presses of the local newspaper, the Southport Visiter, the description ran thus:

"Former visitors to Southport will remember the old Fair Ground, which consisted of dilapidated wooden shanties, Aunt Sallies, coconut shies and so forth. All this rubbish has been cleared away, and what is fittingly termed 'The White City' put in its place. The leading attractions of this new Fair Ground are unquestionably the Figure Eight (nearly a mile in

An aerial view of White City taken in 1920. The Figure Eight is approximately in the same spot as today's Pinfari Wild Cat.

length), the River Caves and the Helter-Skelter. It is unnecessary to dwell on the excitement which may be got out of these particular forms of recreation...altogether the attractions named enable either the visitor or the resident (not excluding the children) to enjoy a very happy hour under the best and most healthy conditions."

After a period of closure during the First World War the desire to build a completely new amusement park on fourteen acres of the Lagoon, now by 1920 under another landfill scheme, was making its mark amongst councillors. The reasons for this further move, when the generally welcomed White City had only recently been established are worthy of investigation. Undoubtedly, the leaders of the town were still preoccupied with maintaining a respectable image and holding popular amusements at arm's length as far as possible. The White City site was somewhat confined, but more importantly, land reclamation on the Foreshore was by no means complete. Here was an opportunity to create something artistic, well away from the elegant Promenade, with ample space for more rides and sideshows, on a well laid out 14-acre site, attractively decorated and designed. This was ideally placed in a new zone, known as 'Princes Park', where other corporation attractions were planned. By 1928, these were a magnificent new open air bathing pool, to be followed by a model yacht pond, a pitch and putt course and an arena for family entertainment. This second move emphasises the main difference between Blackpool Pleasure Beach and Southport's amusement park. Despite the fact that both parks had similar rides, with the same companies operating attractions, the Pleasure Beach had grown as an entirely private enterprise, its success down to a

The station entrance to the Figure Eight Railway was operated by Helters Limited until the end of the 1936 season. The company, partly controlled by Blackpool Pleasure Beach, replaced the ride in 1937, when Charles Paige's Cyclone roller coaster opened on Good Friday of the same year. The claim that the Figure Eight was the longest ride on Pleasureland, and frequently advertised as "Nearly a Mile in Length" in the Southport guidebooks of the time, was one of the many quaint exaggerations of the day. Note in the foreground one of the sleeper paths, which were laid throughout Pleasureland and lasted in part until as late as 1950.

The civic
ceremonial
opening of
Pleasureland
in 1922, as the
mayoral party
savour the
pleasures of
the Whip, then
located on
North Road.
(Photo: Sefton Libraries
Local History Unit,
Southport)

small number of forward-thinking individuals. Southport's ever moving park was planned by the public sector, with private sector operators as tenants, demonstrating that, with enthusiastic officers and councillors, the public sector can be every bit as successful as the private sector in developing tourist attractions.

Completed in time for a 1922 Easter opening, the Liverpool Evening Express of 6 April summed up the excitement of the new amusement park, now called 'Pleasureland':

"Visitors to Southport this Easter-tide will find a complete transformation of the fairground or 'Pleasureland' as it is now called. The Parks and Foreshore Committee of the Corporation have busied themselves throughout the winter in their endeavour to make Southport's 'fun fair' one of the best in the country, and it is held that when Pleasureland is completed their ambition will have been realised...The whole of the grounds have been arranged in a tasteful manner, and the colour scheme of green and white adds considerably to the attractive appearance of the site. Southport has made a big step forward in its publicity scheme, and has now a full-time publicity and attractions manager."

Pond life on the foreshore

Whereas all the major rides from the former White City were moved to new positions within the park, it seems that the Water Chute could not be set up on its site next to the River Caves until the pond had been dug in time for the 1923 season. At the formal opening of Pleasureland by Councillor Aveling on 31 May 1922, so admired was the council's achievement, that a special tribute was paid by Blackpool Councillor WG Bean, who was an honoured guest at the ceremony. He was the man who provided to Blackpool by private enterprise what Southport's Parks and Foreshore Committee had brought about through

The party of distinguished guests at the 1922 official opening of Pleasureland went on to sample a gentle boat ride on the River Caves, the oldest attraction today in Pleasureland, where it has been rebranded and extensively rebuilt as the Lost Dinosaurs of the Sahara.
(Photo: Sefton Libraries Local History Unit, Southport)

In the 1920s there was still an area in Pleasureland as yet undeveloped. This view is from the top of the River Caves looking towards the Runabout, the Figure 8, the Whip and Hiram Maxim's Captive Flying Machine.
(Photo: Sefton Libraries Local History Unit, Southport)

HERE JOY REIGNS SUPREME

The HOUSE of NONSENSE

FORGET DULL CARE
ALL YE WHO ENTER HERE

IF YOU DONT SEE IT
IN THE WINDOW. WE HAVE
IT INSIDE SOMEWHERE. CHILDREN 3D

ADULTS 6D AMUSEMENT INSIDE FOR
SPECTATORS AS PERFORMERS

THERE IS AS MUCH

HOUSE of NONSENSE
3D 6D

The House of Nonsense, seen here shortly after its removal from Southport's White City to the brand new Pleasureland, was a very popular attraction. It was very similar to one operating at Blackpool Pleasure Beach, where a magnificent ultra modern replacement was opened in 1934. Had Leonard Thompson succeeded in taking over Pleasureland in 1939, no doubt he would have commissioned Joe Emberton to build a similar one there. As it was, both funhouses were destroyed by fire; the House of Nonsense did not survive the wartime requisition.

UCKS GOMEZ BALLOON BLOWING

The 1922 official opening of Pleasureland. The civic party poses in front of some of the many sideshows. The sideshows are painted in uniform green and white, a livery which was to last until the end of 1948.

(Photo: Sefton Libraries Local History Unit, Southport)

municipal pride and foresight. The fact that Pleasureland would be a relief rather than a burden on the rates was stressed repeatedly. The Southport Guardian, another local newspaper, reported on the opening ceremony in its edition of 3 June 1922. It described the mayoral party experiencing the Scenic Railway, which had been the talk of Southport, since it first opened without ceremony at Easter. The article went on:

"As a pleasing contrast there is nothing better for a relief than the quietude and beauty of the River Caves." The party rode on the Whip and the Helter-Skelter. The House of Nonsense is described as having "stairs that move about in a most uncanny way, slides and revolving 'terra firma' are some of the features of this device which should not be passed by."

Unlike in Blackpool, Margate's Dreamland and the Kursaal at Southend, Southport Pleasureland did not have a cinema, dancehall, or facilities for mass catering, although it did have four cafes. It also had a multitude of stalls and sideshows, ice cream stands, weighing machines, photo booths such as the 'Scenic Studios' and 'Gerome's' , a household name on Liverpool's London Road. There were palaces of penny slot machines provided by such firms as 'Southport Games Company' where, by turning a handle, photo cards would flick by revealing 'What the Butler Saw' or your palm read electrically as the contours of the hand were explored by ball bearing-style needles moving up and down. A printed card was issued with your 'reading' upon it. There was also an American Bowling Alley, a Kentucky Derby and the 'Skee Ball Alleys', another kind of ball game with tracks, which consisted of bowling balls up a slope into numbered holes. Fortune tellers with their own smart premises were placed amongst stands selling sweets and soft toys. Two new slides with mechanical lifts adorned the grounds, Mrs Uttley's and Mr Houldsworth's 'The Rapids', which was similar to the 'Jack and Jill' at Blackpool, and 'The Big Bowl Slide' alongside the Figure Eight and 'The African Shooting Jungle'.

Pride of place was given to the Scenic Railway, owned and operated by Stephen Hadfield, which ran along the entire southern side of the park. The 1922 Stephenson's Guide to Southport heaped praise on this massive new attraction:

"One of the attractions that makes Pleasureland worthy of the name is the new Scenic Railway which has been constructed for the Scenic Railway (Southport) Limited, by Mr John Monk, engineer, Blackpool, who is also a director of the Company. Mr Monk has had in collaboration with him in the equipment and construction of the railway Messrs Wiseman and Slough of London, who have along with him, been connected with every scenic railway which has been constructed in Europe, and who in great measure were responsible for the construction of a large number of them. The one under review is undoubtedly the highest and longest yet erected. It is driven by an electric motor of 100hp, has automatic signals, comfortable cars, and all the latest up-to-date devices. The sensation of a ride on the Scenic Railway is altogether delightful and exhilarating, and should not be missed by either young or old."

All aboard the caterpillar!

The 100hp electric motor powered the chain on the railway's two inclines – or 'lift hills' as they are now called – first on the inner, higher track and then on the outer lower track which, after passing through the upper portals of the imposing blue painted entrance, began the second circuit. A seated driver in the middle car operated the brake at appropriate moments, dictated by the automatic signals. The train, once freed from the lift hill mechanism, would travel on under its own momentum. Unlike Blackpool's Big Dipper, which opened a year later, it did not have 'under track rollers', so its speed and the ferocity of the drops were restricted. When, three years later, a second scenic railway roller coaster – the Mountain Caterpillar Railway – was opened by the same company, the track of the original Scenic Railway was altered to run through the second portal only. The Caterpillar, with a smaller station but with a similar design, rose to a much greater height, as its lift hill was sandwiched between the double circuits of the Scenic Railway, over which it had to pass. On reaching the summit, it took a right turn to complete three circuits with two large dips in each before entering a rocky tunnel to travel back to the station. The whole edifice provided a dramatic backdrop to the grounds and could be seen from the northernmost point on the Promenade.

From a historical point of view, tribute should be paid today to the foresight and vision of Southport Corporation, whose praiseworthy efforts to improve the town continued with developments up to the outbreak of the 1939–45 war. Now, at the start of the 21st Century, a similar desire by Sefton Council to recreate what they term a 'Classic Resort' recalls the endeavours of 80 years ago.

The Water Chute was a landmark ride at Pleasureland until 1940. Behind the many onlookers in this 1920s view, the structure of the Scenic Railway and the Mountain Caterpillar provide a fitting backdrop. The train high above on the Mountain Caterpillar Railway of 1925 approaches the first dip among the rocks on its three full circuits.
(Photo: Botanic Gardens Museum)

FOUR

~

Looking ahead to Britain's best

In this 1925 shot the Clock Tower entrance has yet to arrive and the arrangement of the sideshows and rides is a little untidy. At this point Pleasureland had three slides all with mechanical stairlifts. The Bowl Slide stands next to the Figure Eight, the Helter Skelter Lighthouse opposite the Runabout and the Alpine Rapids to the right of the Dodgems. (Photo: Robert Preedy Collection)

After the opening of the new site in 1922, Southport Corporation gradually enhanced Pleasureland, firstly by providing a new clock tower entrance in 1926 on the eastern side of the park and, in 1934, constructing the much more spectacular art deco tower entrance facing onto Princes Park.

The Council's Southport Improvement Committee, active from the turn of the century and dedicated to the embellishment of the seafront in general, had kept an eye on developments in other northwest resorts. In 1928 a magnificent open air sea bathing lake with capacity for several thousand spectators, as well as three thousand bathers, was built by the Council to replace the original pool, located on the northern corner of the Marine Drive. This freed a development site, which within two years had become Peter Pan's Pool and Playground, an amusement park for children. However linking the new sea bathing lake with the Promenade was an essential step forward, as to reach the pool it was necessary to walk around the southern perimeter of the Marine Lake or cross by road and bridge next to the Pier.

This is a 1925 view from the top of the Water Chute looking at the many stalls and sideshows in what post-1948 would become the central rides area. The Clock Tower would not be built until 1926. On the left of the pond can be seen the railway sleeper paths which were a feature of both Blackpool Pleasure Beach and Pleasureland in the early days. (Photo: Nick Laister Collection)

By 1923 Pleasureland is in its second year of operation with the Water Chute now a major attraction. The Alpine Slide, or The Rapids as it was also known (left), will move forward to make way for the Mountain Caterpillar in 1925.
(Photo: Nick Laister Collection)

In 1931, a major programme of public works included improvements to the Marine Lake. An attractive Venetian style bridge was opened, straddling two islands within the lake. Coloured lanterns on striped posts in the water, along with white globes and red bulbs, illuminated the bridge. By 1932, tableaux were erected in Pleasureland to complement the neon-lit entrances and rides. The spectacle became attractive enough to qualify as a restrained answer to Blackpool's Illuminations, which had started in full in 1925. Boating on the Marine Lake, with other pleasure craft mingling with the lanterns until late into the evening, was known as 'Venetian Nights' and continued until the outbreak of war in September 1939. Lord Street was equally beautiful with its shop window displays and fairy lights in the trees.

An aerial view circa 1927 of the Pier and, to the left, the original 1914 open air bathing pool. Peter Pan's Pool occupied this site from 1930 after the new sea bathing lake opened in 1928. It was spared the rigours of wartime closure.

(Photo: Sefton Libraries Local History Unit, Southport)

This is a 1929 view of Pleasureland showing, left to right, the Figure Eight, the back of the House of Nonsense, the Helter Skelter Lighthouse, the River Caves, the Mountain Caterpillar and its sister ride, the 1922 Scenic Railway.

(Photo: Stephen Copnall Collection)

An early 1950s view of the Marine Lake and Pleasureland at night. Pre-war this presented a brilliant spectacle, but for reasons unknown, the council did not revive the Venetian Nights.

The animals went in two by two

Pleasureland developed year by year from 1930 onwards, but was hampered by the council's refusal to allow it to open on Sunday. Recovery from the economic depression which hit Liverpool and the Lancashire cotton towns was slow, but Southport was lucky to have a disproportionate number of wealthy residents who kept the shops in business.

In 1930, Hotchkiss Patents, now entirely owned by Blackpool Pleasure Beach, constructed a Noah's Ark on the North Road of Pleasureland. Its American designer, William Homer Strickler, had been in Blackpool since 1921, when he was commissioned to build and design the Noah's Ark on the Pleasure Beach. Whilst the Noah's Ark in Pleasureland was taking

The Noah's Ark in 1949. The pay desk belongs to the 1930s when this style was adopted across Pleasureland. The lamp standard on the left dates from the 1922 opening of the grounds.

shape, Strickler fell as he inspected the site and died in Blackpool a few days later. This new device consisted of a large rocking boat with a house on top with Noah and his animals peering through the open windows. To reach this point as well as to leave, it was necessary to pass various obstacles in dark tunnels, stairs which wobbled and shook and trapdoors on the floor which blew wind or gave you a minor electric shock. A great deal of harmless fun was had by both participants and onlookers. The attraction lasted until 1977 and the much-modernised Noah's Ark at Blackpool Pleasure Beach is still going strong. The opening of a Noah's Ark in Southport was a clear sign of the confidence in Pleasureland felt by Pleasure Beach Managing Director Leonard Thompson. Thompson had taken over the Pleasure Beach reins following the death in 1929 of his father-in-law William Bean, and was clearly committed to the Company continuing to expand its interests in the Council-owned park at Southport.

Helters Limited also introduced a new ride in 1931. This was a conversion of the Helter Skelter Lighthouse, located adjacent to the River Caves, into a Ghost Train. As Helters already operated a Bowl Slide with mechanical stair lift next to the Figure Eight, this was a sensible move. The tower was retained as a landmark to attract custom. The Ghost Train, now on a different site, is still popular today.

In 1930 the Helter Skelter Lighthouse was converted into the Ghost Train. Not until a few years later was the slide removed. The tower remained a landmark for decades. Note the style of the fencing, common to all Helters rides at the time.

The River Caves in the 1920s with the Water Chute to the left. This design of the River Caves survived until the 1970s.

This 1931 panorama shows Pleasureland in all its glory. The colonnades on both sides of the Clock Tower entrance would last until after the 1948 season. Maxim's Flying Machine had another two seasons to go before giving way to the Art Deco tower. The Noah's Ark arrived a year before this picture was taken. (Photo: Nick Laister Collection)

Apart from the Scenic Railway and Mountain Caterpillar, Stephen Hadfield of the Scenic Railway (Southport) Limited managed several other devices on the southern side of the park. These included two roundabouts, an American Dodgem and an Autodrome. The Autodrome was an impressive new ride, consisting of an oval track made up of steel plates through which an electric current passed. This powered a fleet of two-seater cars, which raced along the circuit under steering wheel and pedal accelerator control, operated by the occupant in the driving seat. The current would be switched off after several laps and the cars would slow to a stop, ready for new or repeat riders. Another of Hadfield's devices was the Cake Walk, made up of two gangways which jolted back and forth and up and down to music, emulating the sensation of a stormy sea crossing. Hadfield also operated the Scenic Studios, a photo booth which was very popular at the time.

Farewell to the Flying Machine

In 1931, Stephen Hadfield expanded his Pleasureland operations with the construction of a brand new Motor Speedboat Track on the north side of the park, next to the Water Chute pond and opposite the River Caves and Ghost Train. The concrete 'track' had been dug out and filled with water. For this attraction to function a 500-gallon petrol tank with pump was required. Permission for this was granted by the then Parks, Foreshore and Cemeteries Committee in March 1931.

Helters Limited made the next major move in adding new attractions. Maxim's Flying Machine was removed from the North Road to make way for the Art Deco Entrance, which opened in 1934. This highlighted another difference between Pleasureland and Pleasure Beach. In Southport tenants were kept on short leases, usually just for one or two seasons only. This meant that major rides could go elsewhere or be scrapped altogether, a phenomenon which was to have disastrous consequences in years to come. In the early thirties another Helters ride, The Runabout became The Skooters. This was a more modern form of Dodgem similar to the Autoskooters in Pleasure Beach. These had been manufactured by the Lusse

Brothers, who originally came from Philadelphia, where they produced component parts for cars. Like many other Americans in the amusement industry, they had been drawn to Blackpool. In 1933, they set up a factory under the chairmanship of Leonard Thompson to manufacture rides on site for Pleasure Beach. It was the Lusse brothers who built the Octopus for Blackpool Pleasure Beach in 1937 and the one that arrived in Southport the following year.

In 1936, Helters' plans were coming to fruition in the North Road and seaward end of the park. The House of Nonsense was to remain, but the Figure Eight Railway, the Bowl Slide and

A view in the 1920s. There is a more ordered look to the park. The popular game of Skee-Ball has a prominent position behind the Whip. Pleasureland now has three wooden coasters and by 1931 the Whip and Skee-Ball will have to make way for Stephen Hadfield's Motor Boat Track. This was dug out alongside the Water Chute pond, a corner of which can be seen front right. (Photo: Sefton Libraries Local History Unit, Southport)

The Bowl Slide and African Jungle with the Figure Eight, circa 1936. All three rides made way for the construction of the Cyclone coaster in 1936/37.

Shooting Range were to be pulled down to make way for a much larger roller coaster known as the Cyclone. Charles Paige, a world famous designer of coasters, was commissioned to build this replacement for the Figure Eight. We know from the records that the architect Joseph Emberton, an outstanding exponent of the 'modern movement', designed the station entrance on this ride. He was responsible for the magnificent work being carried out in Blackpool Pleasure Beach, including the Casino building, Fun House and Grand National station. He may have even played a major part in redesigning Pleasureland had everything gone according to plan.

In this 1935 shot the Figure 8 appears in immaculate condition, along with the Noah's Ark and Bowl Slide. The 'Scooters' in the foreground had taken the place of The Runabout.

This is a 1935 view of North Road and the Figure Eight station building. In the foreground some rough ground awaits the arrival of another ride. The mechanical lift to the Bowl Slide awaits its first passengers, as does the Figure Eight.

A 1934 view showing all of Pleasureland with the Marine Drive in the foreground. Helters Figure Eight, on the left, was rather exaggeratedly advertised as being 'nearly a mile in length'. The Art Deco entrance on the extreme left had opened that year. The tunnels of the River Caves run along the perimeter of Pleasureland, freshly painted in white. Next is the Water Chute (demolished in 1940/41) and the Mountain Caterpillar and Scenic Railway, which operated until the close of the 1940 season when the Air Ministry requisitioned the park.
(Photo: Stephen Copnall Collection)

Joseph Emberton's original Cyclone station shortly before the outbreak of war in 1939. Note the design of the station with its uncluttered lines and modern lamps beneath the canopy.

On Good Friday 1937, the Cyclone opened, with an admission of 6d. A much larger structure than anything else in Pleasureland, it was built further out towards the sea over part of the River Caves' tunnels and at the other end right up to the Noah's Ark. The modern track with its steeper dips and driverless trains set a new standard in Pleasureland and a challenge to Stephen Hadfield's Scenic Railway and Mountain Caterpillar on the southern side of the park. In 1938 another two modern rides were erected; the Eli Ferris Wheel and a second Octopus, again owned by Helters. Again, Joseph Emberton's influence could be seen; the entrances to both the Octopus and the 'Eli Ferris Wheel' bore the hallmarks of the 'modern movement' house style adopted at Blackpool Pleasure Beach.

Meanwhile, the Water Chute, dating from 1903, was beginning to show its age and the rapidly worsening international situation from 1938 onwards raised many questions amongst Pleasureland's tenants about the future. By 1938, it is estimated that one third of the attractions now needed updating. In short, massive investment was needed at Pleasureland if the park was to survive and prosper, but this investment was beyond the means of the Council.

The Cyclone blows in

Southport Corporation began to look at how to redesign and modernise the grounds. The Council sought a way of relinquishing control and invited offers from private companies to run the entire park on a single long-term lease. Pressure was also growing from existing tenants and visitors for better and more generous parking facilities for the increasing number of coaches – or charabancs, as they were then called. Indeed the road system from the Southport boundary to Preston and Liverpool had been greatly improved with new dual carriageway bypasses of considerable length, as Lancashire County Council, a pioneer then and still today one of the best authorities in terms of road maintenance and lighting, applied its progressive policies in the 1930s. These developments would have a considerable impact on future thinking and the shape of post war Pleasureland.

A 1952 view of the Octopus which was installed by Helters for the 1938 season.

Stephen Hadfield had been a major force in Pleasureland from its opening in 1922 until requisition after the close of the 1940 season. Like other showmen, he had travelled to the USA for new ideas, and his Scenic Railway of 1922 and the Mountain Caterpillar of 1925 were the most exciting rides in the park until the construction by Helters in 1937 of the Cyclone roller coaster. The whole park had suffered in the trade depression, following the 1929 Wall Street crash and there is evidence that not all stallholders took up tenancies in this period.

Although some new rides were introduced in the 1930s (see above), Southport Corporation focussed its investments elsewhere in the town. The one major exception was the construction of Pleasureland's art deco tower entrance in 1934, which became the most striking icon of the park. At this time, the Council was more concerned with replacing its tram system with luxury buses (December 1934), building new roads in the suburbs, and acquiring the pier in 1936 for modernisation.

It was not until 1937/38 that attention was drawn to what improvements could be made to Pleasureland. At this point Helters, with strong links to Blackpool, was becoming the driving force in Southport's amusement park, whilst at Pleasure Beach a stunning display of modern architecture and up to the minute rides served to underline the progressive nature of developments there.

A rear view of the House of Nonsense, Ghost Train and River Caves in 1934. The sand hills can be seen gradually reaching half way up the tunnels of the River Caves. Windblown sand was always a problem for the rides in this area.

8551. THE LAKE & FLORAL BRIDGE, SOUTHPORT

A 1933 view from the Pier Entrance of the new Venetian Bridge over the Marine Lake where the Venetian Night Spectaculars were held until the outbreak of war in 1939. Middle right can be seen the semi-circular Colonnade where concert parties were held. The whole area was attractively illuminated at night with floodlighting and coloured lanterns and lights. After 1949, when restrictions on public lighting were lifted, the Venetian Lights were never revived. However in 1950 a roller skating rink was established in the Colonnade and later this was moved to a site on Pleasureland on its southern flank adjoining the coach park. (Photo: Sefton Libraries Local History Unit, Southport)

In the period 1937 to 1939, the Publicity and Attractions Committee began to take action on Pleasureland's future. An article appeared in the Southport Visiter on 17 December 1938, which throws some light on the thinking of the time. The article, 'Pleasureland Development – Bringing It Up To Date: Councillor Barber, Publicity Chairman Looks Ahead' was written at what was undoubtedly a highpoint in the history of the town. It ran thus:

"Although Pleasureland has been a very profitable undertaking to the Corporation, the Publicity and Attractions Committee feel that the time has arrived when still further development is needed, and they have decided to invite offers from concessionaires interested in amusement parks to submit tenders for leasing the whole of the land, with the object of making it one of the most attractive amusement parks in Great Britain. I believe Pleasureland, as constructed at present, is obsolete, and at least £20,000 is required to bring it up to date...It is proposed to provide a park for motor coaches other than regular service vehicles, adjacent to Pleasureland. This would, of course, enable passengers travelling by such vehicles conveniently to visit Pleasureland, and this will, in my opinion, be a very valuable arrangement in connection with its future development."

A major player ignored?

Clearly, the council wanted to create a coach park and the only place for that was by relocating the Scenic Railway and Mountain Caterpillar. There had been disagreements over the way leases were now being offered. It seems, with hindsight, that certain lessees were being eased out of Pleasureland. Certainly, a great deal of space had been wasted in the 1922 layout of the grounds. The two large banks of sideshows effectively closed off several acres, which could have been used for new rides or other attractions. From council minutes, we know that Stephen Hadfield, who had as strong a presence on Pleasureland as Helters, was being offered different sites from those he had occupied.

Blackpool Pleasure Beach was prestigious, financially powerful and had maintained an excellent business profile in difficult trading conditions. Its clientele was drawn from all social classes in the north. It is hardly surprising that in 1939 Southport Corporation would immediately shortlist the Pleasure Beach when considering bids from Butlin's and from the existing stallholders and ride operators from Pleasureland, because the Thompson family had proved what they could achieve. Stephen Hadfield's overtures, and those of the stallholders with no connection to Blackpool, were given short shrift, leading to a sense of unease amongst them.

In December 1937, Stephen Hadfield had made an application to the corporation for new leases on various devices at Pleasureland, including the Scenic Railway and Caterpillar. He backed up this application with a promise to spend considerable sums of money on bringing his rides up-to-date, as well as helping to re-construct the fairground as a whole. However, the corporation was only prepared to extend current agreements by 12 months and this was followed by a decision to defer Hadfield's subsequent request to install a Moon Rocket ride at the park. Given the fact that Hadfield was such a significant operator, whose rides included two wooden coasters, as well as roundabouts, a set of dodgems and a motor boat track, it is hardly surprising that he felt he was being ignored.

FIVE

⁓

From hope to war

North Road in 1941. The Cyclone station is being mothballed for a period of requisition of indefinite length. At the end of North Road a last look at the House of Nonsense, soon to be destroyed by fire.

In 1939, Southport Corporation grasped the most significant opportunity to develop Pleasureland for many years. It had drawn up a 30-year lease giving Mr Leonard Thompson of Blackpool Pleasure Beach complete control of the amusement park. The deal was due to be signed on 1 November 1939 and the new arrangement was already being referred to as 'The Southport Pleasure Beach Company Limited'. Council minutes of July in that year record a letter from Southport Chamber of Trade asking the Town Council to give protection to the present tenants and their families in any future arrangements. In August the Southport Hotel and Apartments Association "noted with satisfaction the proposals for the transformation and improvement of Pleasureland".

These were indeed words of praise and we know that Joseph Emberton had exciting plans including a casino building similar to the one in Blackpool. He is quoted as saying that he wanted to create "a beautiful garden, fitted up as an amusement park." Signs of Emberton's magic touch could be seen post war in the design of the reopened Helters attractions when Leonard Thompson had every reason to believe that he would shortly be taking over.

Gravity and caution

An article in the fairground trade newspaper, World's Fair, of 15 April 1939 paints a unique picture of the time. Under the headline 'Southport Pleasureland Reopens Good Friday Holiday Crowds', the writer, Frederick H-U Bowman (who one assumes is American), writes:

"The Good Friday re-opening of Pleasureland at Southport attracted a lot of people, and the general impression was that business equalled expectations. On all sides, however, I heard that the gravity of the international political situation was making the public cautious about spending money.

"Moreover, there is talk about the site of Pleasureland being offered in its entirety for acquisition by some amusement caterer, so many tenants feel discouraged from making improvements for fear the ground changes hands and their efforts prove futile. Helters, however, having invested in new rides such as the Cyclone seemed more positive.

"Mr Ayling [manager of Helters' rides at Pleasureland] is one of the optimists who goes ahead regardless of war scares and rumours. Already his attractions have been internally repainted and renovated, including all the beautiful tableaux in the round-the-world water caves, and the exteriors are now being tackled. Moreover he has installed two fresh rides – an Octopus with bright yellow cars and a large Ferris Wheel. His immense Noah's Ark – a building, not a roundabout ride – was rocking in the supposed flood, with an elephant, a giraffe and other animals aboard, while Noah himself was fishing over the side, accompanied by his wife. A huge shark, with a fearsome array of teeth, was awaiting its next meal. The figures are all animated by mechanical movement, and two big pelicans keep opening their beaks.

"The mammoth scenic set depicting an oriental palace, with its vista of bathing pools, looked picturesque and impressive, while the Ghost Train now has an illuminated figure of

In this picture from 1923 the Scenic Railway stands in a commanding position before the advent of the Mountain Caterpillar, which rather hid it from view. The structure would be fully revealed again during the 1941–46 Air Ministry requisition. The Scenic Railway was the only ride on the south side of Pleasureland to survive intact this extremely damaging period in its history.

death on the footplate, as well as a lighted skull, revealed at intervals by a sliding panel. Happy parties were revelling in the switchback railway (sic), where Mr Ayling has introduced powerful new floodlights for night illumination...the House of Nonsense was also well patronised.

"There were plenty of palmists, and for three shies a penny, visitors had the choice of two bulls-eyes, guaranteed to drop a man in the ducking pond. The crowds amused themselves also at the rifle range with the moving targets. Descriptions of lost children are written on a large blackboard. Kelly's Wedding still tempts the mischievous to knock off the gentlemen's top hats. The cafes seemed busy, and the Wall's ice-cream tricycles were well patronised at the entrance, while the Lakeside Miniature Railway claimed its quota of passengers."

On the outbreak of war, Southport Corporation's Publicity and Attractions Committee decided to retain control of Pleasureland for the time being, but granted Mr Thompson an option to take up the 30-year lease on November 1st next, following cessation of hostilities, "or such earlier date as may be agreed".

After an initial closure of all places of entertainment nationally, the government allowed a considerable relaxation of restrictions, as the atmosphere of the phoney war took hold. Arrangements were set in hand for the 1940 season and the Council renewed leases with its existing tenants, albeit with some difficulty due to resentment and a feeling of uncertainty amongst many in Pleasureland. As we know, Leonard Thompson was about to sign on the dotted line when the outbreak of war put a stop to everything. Stephen Hadfield was given a one-year lease to operate his rides for the 1940 season.

Both pre-war and in early post-war years the area around Pleasureland was mainly undeveloped with unspoilt sand dunes. These were ideal for picnickers who could hire Corporation deckchairs.
(Photo: Sefton Libraries Local History Unit, Southport)

Requisition and disaster for all

From a historical perspective, there is no doubt that the Council had made the right decision in its negotiations with Blackpool Pleasure Beach, but it had needlessly upset those who wanted to play a part in the modernisation of the park in cooperation with Mr Thompson. In fact, disaster was looming for all concerned as, in the end, none of the parties came to an agreement and a fantastic opportunity would be lost for decades.

The 1940 season at Pleasureland commenced on Good Friday, 22 March. All the rides were fully operational, but permission had been given to the Southport Boating Company to dismantle the Water Chute at the end of September. At the request of Leonard Thompson, the pond into which the boats plunged would be retained for future development. Mr Stephen Hadfield had also signalled his intention to remove certain of his devices, fuelled it would seem by his deteriorating relationship with the council. By August 1940, the Battle of Britain was at its height. Nobody in Southport was giving much thought to the 1941 season as the council decided not to publish a new edition of the Southport Official Guide Book for 1941–42.

The Town Clerk received a letter, dated 21 December 1940, from the Air Ministry requisitioning the whole area of Pleasureland, and the triangular piece of land outside Pleasureland, used as a car park. By March 1941, barriers and fencing were being erected from the Esplanade to the Marine Drive, isolating the entire park where aeroplane parts were to be stored, hidden amongst the silent rides. All tenants and lessees were prevented from operating in

A 1947 picture of the Cyclone in its original state before the remodelling of the sideshows, which can just be seen on the right.

Pleasureland, and the entire park remained closed for the next three seasons from 1941 to 1943 inclusive. Only the Lakeside Miniature Railway carried trippers in its steam trains to Pleasureland station, still operating outside the barrier. To peer through the wire at the ghostly, silent world of the amusements of yesteryear was the only attraction on offer. The return ticket on the train took passengers back to the Pier station.

The Pier had also been closed, carrying as it did at its seaward end searchlights to catch enemy bombers flying above on their way to Bootle and Liverpool, destined to become the most heavily bombed conurbation outside London. From Ainsdale northwards, anti-invasion wooden posts were hammered into the entire Southport beach at low tide to prevent gliders or planes from landing on the beach, although people were not prevented from going onto the shore.

Amidst the requisitioning of many hotels and other public buildings at this time, and indeed the not insignificant air raids on Southport itself, one oasis was to remain open, the children's paradise of Peter Pan's Pool and Playground. Here the Jungle Train, the Jigsaw Railway and the Wendy Glide, the Dive Bomber and the slides and swings on the sandy enclosure carried on their task of bringing happiness to countless wartime children. A place where you could still drink a bottle of pop with a portion of chips and feel a million miles away, for a day at least, from the grey atmosphere of the blitzed cities.

In Pleasureland itself, the presence of fuselages and other aeroplane parts meant that tenants could not access the park, bringing damage and decay to its infrastructure and claims for compensation for loss of earnings from Stephen Hadfield and other tenants. At the request of the Air Ministry, the Mountain Caterpillar Railway was dismantled and stored. Helters House of Nonsense burnt down and was not replaced. The River Caves and the Cyclone became silted up from the unrelenting windblown sand. A very high tide was also capable of doing damage to the rides where access to all unauthorised persons was strictly forbidden and where only official photographs, taken on the eve of requisition, provided a record of what once had been. The deterioration slowly set in, particularly some of the colonnades on either side of the clock tower which began to sag.

Normality returns – for some

This occupation of the park would last for three and a half seasons. Then, in July 1944, following the Normandy invasion and with an end to war in sight, the public regained access to Pleasureland, although only a quarter of the park was open to them. This reopening only benefited Helters and Hotchkiss Patents (i.e. those associated with Blackpool Pleasure Beach), as their rides dominated this section of the park.

From the Art Deco Tower entrance in Princes Park along the North Road past Noah's Ark to the far end of the Cyclone Coaster, the sideshows and Peggy's Café plus half a dozen rides were operating. The yellow cars of the Octopus and the dizzying loops of the Dive Bomber were drawing the crowds, but the longest queues were for the Cyclone. Elsewhere on the park, onlookers laughed as girls screamed, their skirts billowing as a last blast of air ejected them from Noah's Ark. Pleasureland was back in action!

A little further down North Road, the Ducking Pond, or Bull's Eye sideshow as it was known, had gathered a large crowd as a long-suffering man fell into the water each time the target above him was hit. Peace had returned, if only for a day, to those enjoying themselves in the park.

1948 and a real steam locomotive 'King George V' draws a well loaded train around the newly opened curve from the Marine Drive Station on its way to Pleasureland. (Photo: Sefton Libraries Local History Unit, Southport)

Presenting a silent spectacle of what once had been, the rest of Pleasureland remained fenced off. The Clock Tower Entrance, the Scenic Railway, the many sideshows which had survived the three and a half years of Air Ministry occupation, the Water Chute pond, the Motor Boat track, the River Caves and large empty spaces where rides such as the Mountain Caterpillar Railway and the Water Chute itself once stood, completely dwarfed the small area now operating.

Nevertheless, with the town full of servicemen, American soldiers from nearby bases and government employed workers relocated to the North West, there was no shortage of customers.

The council reopened Pleasureland for the full 1945 season, but still only the portion which had functioned in the latter part of 1944. The tally of rides operated by Helters Limited was the Cyclone, the Ghost Train, the Octopus and the Eli Ferris Wheel. Hotchkiss Patents from Blackpool Pleasure Beach had installed the Dive Bomber on the site of the burnt down House of Nonsense and had already, the year before, reopened the 1930 Noah's Ark. A Dodgem Track, a Cake Walk and a Kiddies Roundabout, with the sideshows on North Road, completed what was on offer. The rest of the park remained closed. The Scenic Railway, silhouetted against the maritime skies, stood silent, but to the uninitiated observer it was surely about to burst back into life, as soon as all of Pleasureland emerged from its frozen state.

PLEASURELAND
SOUTHPORT
1947 Features
THE CYCLONE COASTER
The Latest and Most Up-to-Date Ride in the World
RIVER CAVES
Always New! Always Changed!! Always Enlarged!!!
THE GHOST TRAIN
FULL OF NEW SURPRISES
THE OCTOPUS
THREE RIDE SENSATIONS IN ONE
ELI FERRIS WHEEL
SAFE FOR YOUNG AND OLD
NOAH'S ARK
ALWAYS A FAVOURITE
THE DIVE BOMBER
THE LATEST THRILL

Helters and Hotchkiss Patents advertised their attractions at Pleasureland in this format from the mid 1920s until the end of the 1950s.

In this 1946 shot the railway sleeper paths take our eyes to the new Dive Bomber of that year and, alongside, the 1938 Eli Ferris Wheel. The windmill of the River Caves is turning again between the Eli Wheel and the freshly painted tower of the Ghost Train (once the Helter Skelter Lighthouse), after five years of inactivity.

For the lessees, there was still immense uncertainty. For two seasons, in 1944 and 1945, Stephen Hadfield earned no income from Pleasureland, as the southern side of the park was not released until 1946. On 18th January 1946, before the whole of Pleasureland had enjoyed a single season of full operation, negotiations between Leonard Thompson and Southport Corporation resumed. Due to the ongoing uncertainty over his future at the park, and the four to five years of lost revenue, Stephen Hadfield decided to dispose of the Scenic Railway and Mountain Caterpillar roller coasters, the former of which was still standing. He put them on sale early in 1946. One assumes Blackpool Pleasure Beach was not interested, even though the rides were in good condition. Eventually showman John Collins purchased the coasters and rebuilt them within months at Sutton Great Park amusement park at Sutton Coldfield.

Unpleasant surprises and missed opportunities

The period 1946 to 1948 was a time of unpleasant surprises and missed opportunities. Although in 1946 the whole of Pleasureland was open for business, the beloved Scenic Railway had gone forever with no sign at all of any attempt to replace it. The electric speed-way, the Autodrome, was the only one of Stephen Hadfield's rides to survive, now standing in the shadow of the Clock Tower Entrance. It too would disappear after two seasons. Yes, it was good – very good – that the River Caves, cleared of sand, was now in full swing, that the Motor Speedway was running along the former Motor Boat Track and that the Water Chute pond had become the new home for those motor boats. Nothing however could compensate for the grievous loss of the 1922 Scenic Railway, which had been the star attraction for many years, ever since the opening of the park on its current site. An almost identical coaster still operates under listed status today in Margate's Dreamland Amusement Park, but at the time of writing its future is also uncertain. In the case of the Southport Scenic, the unavailability of timber in this immediate post-war period must have been a factor in the removal of the ride.

The war had changed everything in Britain. A new post-war government had as its priorities the rebuilding of the country, particularly houses and factories. All materials were strictly rationed. In addition, new policies such as the Green Belt and the Town and Country Planning Act restricted the freedom of any commercial development. These restrictions would remain in force until the mid-fifties. Dim-out rather than blackout was the order of the day, particularly in the winter of 1946/47 in what felt like an increasingly impoverished Britain.

Was this the reason why Southport Corporation did not immediately follow through its promise to sign a deal with Blackpool Pleasure Beach on 1 November 1945 after cessation of hostilities, as had been agreed in 1939? Or was it that Pleasureland, in its damaged state, with a ragbag of sideshows along railway sleeper paths that (with the exception of North Road) now led to nowhere, no longer looked like such an attractive proposition, especially given all the acute shortages of materials? Or did the council attempt to drive too hard a bargain? Whereas pre-war it had almost been possible to think of Pleasureland with its three coasters and many equivalent or duplicate rides to Blackpool as in the same league as the Pleasure Beach, this was certainly no longer the case in 1946. The fact that the park was council owned, with several different tenants, was almost certainly the main reason for this.

Leonard Thompson had been able to keep his Blackpool park fully operational throughout the war and was now in a much stronger position as a bidder for complete control in

The motor boats and River Caves in an early post-war view. The picture would remain much the same until the mid-1950s when the Ferris Wheel and the Dive Bomber were briefly replaced by a Moon Rocket.

In this 1946 shot the pier has re-opened after its wartime closure as strollers make their way towards the sea. The tram service of the time started well short of the entrance. It was replaced in the early 1950s by a miniature railway, built by Harry Barlow, and ran the full length of the structure. (Photo: Southport Visiter)

The Cyclone was an immediate hit when it opened in 1937. It has survived many twists of fate and is still a major draw at Pleasureland. This early post-war picture shows the original train on the last dip. (Photo: Nick Laister Collection)

Southport. A rival bid from Billy Butlin had been rejected and the evidence from council minutes suggests that any overtures from Mr Stephen Hadfield and the other tenants had, for reasons best known to the council of the time, been given the cold shoulder.

Mr Thompson clears the field

Mr Thompson attended a meeting of the Publicity and Attractions Committee in Southport on 18 January 1946 where it was resolved "that negotiations be re-opened with Blackpool Pleasure Beach Limited for a lease of Pleasureland on the lines referred to in the minute 2719 of this committee of the 20 July 1939, subject to reconsideration of the financial terms". It appeared that the field was clear. An article appeared in the Southport Visiter announcing a £100,000 investment plan for the park, but did not give specific details.

Stephen Hadfield must have sensed a vacuum in the Council's handling of matters at this time. With the proceeds from the sale of the Scenic Railway and Mountain Caterpillar, he was actually in a position to invest in new rides for Pleasureland. In a letter of 15 October 1947, realising that negotiations with Blackpool Pleasure Beach were taking longer than they should, Hadfield offered to manage Pleasureland for the Corporation or take a lease of Pleasureland. This offer was not accepted. By the end of the 1947 season, having sold his final

A 1947 view of that part of Pleasureland, mostly under Helters' control, which had best survived the period of requisition 1941–44. The Water Chute pond, minus the Water Chute, is now a lake for motor boats and the track next to it has been drained to make a Motor Speedway.

A 1947 view of Helters' attractions on North Road Pleasureland. Note the perfect symmetry of the freshly painted Cyclone Coaster after its wartime hibernation.

remaining ride (the Autodrome), Hadfield had relinquished all his interests in Pleasureland. His relationship with Southport Corporation had deteriorated. Sadly, after a most valuable contribution over many years, he retired from the amusement park scene and became a farmer, which was a very lucrative business in the Southport area.

By 1948, negotiations with Blackpool Pleasure Beach had also gone adrift and were on the point of stalling completely, much to the annoyance of Leonard Thompson. In council minutes of 6 September 1948, these negotiations were referred to as "concluded". Blackpool, through its company Hotchkiss Patents, now merely controlled the Noah's Ark and Dive Bomber and, through its shares in Helters Limited, an interest in the rides of that company.

SIX

A peak in popularity

Towards the end of 1948, the Borough Engineer drew up a scheme of public works to improve the state of Pleasureland and rationalise its design, appropriate to the altered post-war circumstances. The council gave permission to proceed and, at once, the colonnades were demolished and replaced with brick walls, the southern third of the park was destined to become a coach park with a tarmac surface and the central area widened and then resurfaced to form a new rides area. Without the Scenic Railway, the straggling remnants of the stalls leading there were removed and the sideshows along North Road, and on one side only of the new central area, were rebuilt to a uniform design of green and cream with red lettering. From the start of the 1949 season, an arcade provided a through route from one side of the sideshow block to the other. This scheme made a much better use of space than the wasteful layout pre-war. With decorative lighting restrictions lifted from April 1949, Pleasureland became much busier and more attractive at night, not closing until 10.30 pm.

In the new central area were the Caterpillar, the Galloping Horses and the leaning Crazy Cottage. There was, however, still a feeling of a half-finished plan on the southern side of the central area, as there was no continuous row of rides or sideshows at this point to delineate the limits of the amusement park. A policy of no duplication of rides was adopted by the

A 1949 view of Pleasureland. Behind the Art Deco tower the Cyclone is the main attraction, now that more than a third of the pre-war rides have disappeared. The River Caves left with its castle turrets and windmill has remained unchanged since 1922.

(Photo: Nick Laister Collection)

council, so each addition to the fairground had to be different. Anyone who had last visited Pleasureland in 1948 noticed a considerable improvement.

Amphibious invasion

The Lakeside Miniature Railway, extended beyond the Pier to Peter Pan's Pool, now linked the two amusement parks, bringing plenty of custom to both destinations and to two new corporation attractions which were based at the intersection of the Pier and the Marine Drive. These were open top buses which ran over the sands to Ainsdale Beach and back and amphibious vehicles known as DUKWs, acquired from the Army and which took trippers out to sea.

As the 1940s turned into the 1950s, Southport had reached something of a peak in its popularity as a seaside resort. The Marine Lake was alive again with boats of every kind. The Pier

The Pier Entrance was renamed the Casino when the pier re-opened after its wartime closure. In the years immediately prior to the outbreak of war it had been an amusement centre and small funfair.

It's 1950 and Southport is on the brink of a golden decade for the holiday trade. The guides of the time were very well crafted and full of detail.

was open, but not yet extended. There was roller skating in the Colonnade to the strains of the 'Nickel Odeon' and aquatic displays and beauty contests in the Sea Bathing Lake. There was 'Moonlight Bathing' in the floodlit pool and open air dancing under the coloured lights of Lord Street Bandstand. Cinemas, theatres, concert parties and dancing at the Floral Hall added to the attractions. All of this made Southport a very pleasant place in which to spend a holiday. The 1950s were good years for a town of which its inhabitants could be justly proud.

In 1950, Pleasureland had reached a point in its history where it would not greatly change until the advent of the 1970s. A Helter Skelter, later to become the Bowl Slide, had joined its ranks. However, Southport Corporation was still pursuing its aim of major development. This plan was regularly mentioned in the official guidebooks of the time. A design competition was launched for the country's architects to come up with a suitable answer. Not one of these efforts came to fruition, but the Aerial Cableway was erected after the removal in 1974/75 of the Art Deco and Clock Tower entrances and also the position of the coach park became permanent.

Art Deco Entrance and view along Pleasureland's North Road, circa 1950. The Octopus (1938), Noah's Ark (1930) and the Cyclone (1937) reopened in mid-summer 1944, but the Motor Speedway (top left), created by draining the 1931 Motor Boat Track, did not open until 1946 when the rest of Pleasureland was released from Air Ministry requisition.

What might have been: For a number of years during the 1950s, Southport Corporation invited leading architects to produce new design and development plans for Pleasureland. This one incorporates many rides of the time and bears the influence of the 1951 Festival of Britain.

In 1951, the year of the Festival of Britain, the fairground showman John Collins removed his Scenic Railway – relocated from Pleasureland in 1946 – from Sutton Park and rebuilt it as the 'Big Dipper' in Battersea Pleasure Gardens. Ironically, this ride, the origins of which had been in Southport, lived on in London, until in 1972 when a tragic accident, with several fatalities, forced its closure.

The Dragon Ride at Battersea, which had been created out of some of Southport's stored Mountain Caterpillar, which had also been sold to John Collins, operated for the 1951 season only. John Collins then moved it to Seaburn in Sunderland where it was rebuilt as the Big Dipper. It operated there from 1952 to 1970, when a fatal accident closed the ride permanently.

SEVEN

Changing times and a struggle to survive

In 1955, a successful application was made to construct a Fun House next to the Bowl Slide. This continued the line of rides marking the southern boundary with the new coach park. In 1955, the Dive Bomber was replaced by a Moon Rocket, which may have originated in Blackpool, where a similar ride ceased operation in 1953. Helters had also found that neither the Ferris Wheel nor the Octopus were attracting enough custom. The Octopus therefore gave way to the Hurricane Jets in time for the 1956 season and, in 1961, the more exciting Flying Saucers rotating above a revolving platform filled the gap left by the removal of the Eli Ferris Wheel five years earlier.

By 1955 children had their own version of a coaster. In the background the Dodgems, Ghost Train tower and River Caves.

A 1950s view of the River Caves entrance which remained very much the same from 1922 until 1978.

Right: It's 1955 and the Wheel and Dive Bomber have gone. A new artistic touch has been added to the tower of the Ghost Train. It seems as if the Moon Rocket was an inadequate replacement for its predecessors and only lasted a few years before it gave way to the Haunted Swing and 1001 Mirrors.

Below: A 1952 night scene at Pleasureland, looking across the Octopus, Cake Walk, River Caves and Ferris Wheel.

In 1956 the Hurricane Jets replaced the less popular Octopus, which too often induced nausea in its passengers. These Jets proved to be one of the most popular of Helters' rides for three decades.

Above left: Erecting the new Flying Saucers Big Wheel ride in time for the 1961 season. An identical wheel opened at Pleasureland in 2005.

Above right: The revolving platform of the Flying Saucers nears completion in front of the 1001 Mirrors, Haunted Swing and the Juvenile Autodrome, where the Moon Rocket once stood.

How about you? We're off to the zoo!

An important development alongside Pleasureland was the establishment of a zoo and pets corner. In March 1953, permission was given by the council to Mr FN Farrar, "for a building proposed to be erected on the site adjoining Pleasureland, for the establishment of a Children's Zoo". This was a strategic site by the Art Deco Entrance and only yards away from the Lakeside Miniature Railway station. It was a development very much in line with the tradition of locating zoos adjacent to amusement parks, a tradition started by Manchester's Belle Vue, which was as famous for its zoo as it was for its large funfair rides, such as the Scenic Railway and sensational Bobs Coaster. Indeed, for a number of years in the 1980s, Pleasureland was marketed as "Amusement Park and Zoo", before it just became "The Amusement Park on the Sands".

Another new attraction opened near to Pleasureland in 1956. A charming model village, known as the 'Land of the Little People' was opened by local Southport family the Dobbins. By 1957, it was in full swing and became an extremely popular venue, later to be cruelly sacrificed to an aborted shopping scheme.

The large number of stallholders on Pleasureland remained constant throughout the 1950s and 1960s, but there were fewer stallholders now than in the pre-war period. The area occupied by sideshows had been made much more compact in the remodelling of 1949/50 and, by the mid-1950s, it was becoming clear that rides were a bigger draw. Whilst such attractions as the Kentucky Derby, Skittles, Cup Smashers and the Shooting Range retained their popularity alongside the palmists and clairvoyants, some sideshow owners put their rented spaces to new uses. A Hall of Mirrors opened in 1950 near the Octopus ride and remained there for decades. Bingo took over from ball games, Hoop-la and the like. The most iconic stall of all, going back to the pre-First World War White City days when the park was on the south side of Marine Lake, was the Bull's Eye (or Ducking Pond). This attraction made a final exit from Pleasureland at the close of the 1956 season after the tenant, Mr W Ball, applied to the council for a change of use. The Bull's Eye had always been a major crowd

In this 1954 shot the tide laps the low wall of the Marine Drive in front of the sea bathing lake, with its landmark globe. Twenty years later the area in front of the Cyclone would be occupied by a slide park called 'Sportsland'.

(Photo: Klaus Gloede, Berlin)

The Black Hole building houses a 'skid' ride. The cars are made to 'skid' by the rider pressing a pedal inside the car.

(Photo: Nick Laister)

When the Dive Bomber and Eli Ferris Wheel were removed from Pleasureland, the Swing Boats and the Moon Rocket took their place for a few years, before the more permanent structure of the '1001 Mirrors' was installed. This shot shows the Swingboats in 1955.

puller on North Road for visitors on their way to the Noah's Ark. No more would the crowds be able to watch the unfortunate man drop into the water each time the bull's eye was hit. Tenants were given little security or encouragement by the council landlords and stalls could change hands after twelve months, so short were their leases.

As the 1950s progressed, heralding increased prosperity, the central rides area gradually became more crowded with, on average, at least one additional device every other season. Here too were the first signs of pleasant landscaping which, on a vastly increased scale, has made Pleasureland so much more attractive since 1990. Today's Black Hole started life in the late 1950s as the Swirl. Cars ran on a circular platform and, by use of a pedal in the car, customers could make the car whip. It was later renamed the 'Supersonic Skid' and has now become the dark ride we know today opposite the Funhouse.

Once Sunday opening was permitted from mid-1954 onwards and with many more transportable devices, rather than the much larger but less numerous permanent rides of the 1920s and 1930s, Pleasureland's takings were given a boost. The park also continued to remain open until 10.30pm.

Pleasureland changed little in the 1950s and 1960s. One device which flourished in the sixties was the Trabant, or Satellite, a revolving platform which lifted, tilted and whirled its passengers in the shadow of the Clock Tower Entrance. The children's Minitrain, which also survives today as the Marrakech Express, made its appearance in the same decade.

For nearly two decades the northern corner of Pleasureland was the most permanent part of the grounds. This 1967 view is from the Noah's Ark.

In the winter of 1960/61 a hurricane force storm severely damaged the Cyclone. It was quickly rebuilt in time for the start of the 1961 season. Looking towards Marine Drive on a gloomy winter's day.

The Art Deco entrance, pictured here in the early 1970s, was one of the most enduring iconic structures of the park. Its demolition in 1974 weakened the appearance of the park's north eastern entrance.
(Photo: Stephen Copnall)

Too little, too late?

As the 1970s approached it was becoming clear that Southport would have to look at the profile of its holiday clientele and respond accordingly, if it were to survive as a resort. That this response would be too little and too late was exacerbated by the fact that in 1974 Southport Corporation would no longer exist. This was to be a turning point in the town's history. No one was sure what the town's fate would be when it lost many of the advantages of local services run within a coherent county borough. When Southport became part of Sefton, transport became the responsibility of the Merseyside Passenger Transport Executive. The main gain for the town was the securing of the busy electric railway link along the coast to Liverpool, which unbelievably had been threatened with closure by Dr Beeching's accountants. The cheap fares that came with the Executive, one of the most progressive and forward-looking in the UK, saved the line. The change from a resort where people stayed for a week, when there were plenty of different attractions to visit each day, to a venue for day-trippers had already begun.

The 'cotton towns' (the busy manufacturing towns of the north west of England) had also radically changed in character. Southport was (and still is) one of the pleasantest towns in England and could at this point have gone over to being almost entirely residential, with the slow rundown and eventual closing of its holiday attractions. Indeed, to a certain extent, this

Band concerts and beauty contests were staple fare in the Southport of the 1950s and 1960s.

In the 1970s car ownership was not universal and many trippers came to Pleasureland by coach. The Clock Tower entrance can clearly be seen, but also the truncated nature of the park since re-modelling in 1949.

happened with the loss of the open-air pool and Peter Pan's Pool and Playground/Happiland two decades later. A period of decay and neglect set in, not immediately obvious to those who only left their cars when at their destination, but increasingly dispiriting to those who cared about what they saw as they walked along the paths and marine parks, so carefully tended before. Innumerable plans and much publicised schemes littered the pages of the local press, but came to nothing, thus engendering an 'I'll believe it when I see it' cynicism. For many years, a threat of demolition hung over Southport Pier.

The 1970s also saw New Brighton's fortunes decline when the ferry link with Liverpool's Pier Head was removed and, shortly after, the pier demolished and the popular Tower Amusement Park and Ballroom razed to the ground. No wonder, then, that its day-trippers increasingly turned to Southport, a very convenient half an hour away by bus, car or train. Already it was evident that noticeably fewer people, other than the conference trade, were staying in the town's hotels and boarding houses, but the number of shoppers and day visitors was steadily increasing.

Indeed, Pleasureland's coach park bore witness to this, as buses with full passenger loads arrived daily from East Lancashire and the West Midlands to the welcoming arms of the amusement park. Busy by day, Pleasureland was much less active at night, a factor that would become even more marked as the years passed. The 1970s was a period in which many traditional amusement parks, both coastal and inland, closed their doors. Some doom-laden voices amongst stallholders and ride-operators forecast its eventual demise as had happened at Southend's Kursaal and Battersea's Festival Gardens. Fortunately, the north was different, more traditional, and – in Southport's case – not lacking in people who wanted the town to thrive. There were problems, as the fate of Belle Vue and New Brighton at that time illustrated, but there were also hopeful signs, of which more in the next chapter.

EIGHT

A search for a new identity

The Clock Tower entrance in 1971. Madame Adele, clairvoyant, has her premises here. Palmists were part and parcel of the traditional seaside amusement park, which Pleasureland then was. Southport Rock is also on sale (left) and through the arch we can see the Satellite on lift-off and the topsy-turvy roof of the Crazy Cottage.
(Photo: Stephen Copnall)

At the beginning of the 1970s, it was clear that investment was needed for Pleasureland to continue as the major holiday attraction in Southport. Some rides were beginning to show their age and, without renovation, would probably close, so strict were the safety standards, which were rigidly enforced.

Already aware that Southport Corporation's days were drawing to a close, the tenants and lessees would have to deal with a new landlord by 1974. At this time, Helters Limited, under the direction of Ted Ayling, had the honour of being the longest serving company in the park. Ted succeeded his late father in 1950, having started work on the Pleasureland Figure Eight Railway as a bellboy, counting the number of people who took repeat rides. His office was in a bungalow set amongst the track of the Cyclone, a ride he helped to build.

Ted's efforts at Pleasureland were eventually recognised when he collected an award in recognition of his services to the amusement park industry from Buckingham Palace.

In 1971 the Mini-Train was an early example of what could be achieved by landscaping and placing models of animals between the tracks.
(Photo: Stephen Copnall)

Behind the Hurricane Jets a train on the Cyclone travels up the first lift-hill in 1971. In the foreground Silcocks have taken over the Motor Speedway and Motor Boat lake from Maxwell Manners & Pring, who, by this time, had left Peter Pan's Pool and Pleasureland altogether.
(Photo: Stephen Copnall)

The Flying Saucers were first installed at Pleasureland in 1961. The Helters Limited Group had a monopoly of rides since 1922 in this part of the park. (Photo: Stephen Copnall)

Silcock's Motor Speedboats on the Boating Lake in 1971. The old Water Chute pond has been reduced in size to accommodate the Astroglide. Space was at a premium from the 1970s onwards. (Photo: Stephen Copnall)

Jackson's of Congleton operated a very popular Waltzer on Pleasureland until 2003.

Ted Ayling (second left) with his wife and colleagues from Pleasureland. The location, in Bibby Road, Churchtown, is where Mr and Mrs Ayling are being given a send-off on their way to a Buckingham Palace garden party. Mr Ayling's service to the amusement park industry from the 1930s until the 1980s was recognised in this way.

(Photo: Peter Raymond Photography, Southport)

Another major player was Silcock Brothers, part of a well established showman and fairground family (today operating as Silcock Leisure). Silcocks had taken over the Motor Boat Lake from Maxwell, Manners and Pring and divided it into two, with 'Whirlaboats' in one half and the conventional motor boats in the other. Silcocks also began to expand into catering and amusement arcades in other parts of the town and elsewhere on the Lancashire coast. They were ready to erect major rides, some with continental European origins, and were prepared to alter the grounds to accommodate them.

Jacksons of Congleton, who ran a Waltzer near the Bowl Slide, were also present on the park. They were well-known in the amusement industry as manufacturers of fairground devices and had a good relationship with the council. Another company with interests on Pleasureland, from 1975 to 1986, was the Sunnysands Leisure Group, which operated the aerial cableway, the 'Sky Ride'. The Sky Ride station was built on the site of the demolished Art Deco entrance and the ride ran along the full length of the eastern side of the grounds. The company's executive, Jeremy Meade, finally left Southport to concentrate on his caravan business in Wales.

Which way to turn?

At one point in the 1970s, the affairs of Pleasureland could have gone in a number of directions. Southport enjoys well above average hours of sunshine and always attracts plenty of day-trippers for this reason. Silcocks particularly saw the potential of the resort and by 1970 had already erected a multi-lane slide over part of the boating lake. In 1973, they converted

Silcock's Whirl-A-Round, pictured here in 1971, was a popular ride for several decades, positioned beyond the Fun House, which modestly called itself at the time "the best in the world".
(Photo: Stephen Copnall)

1971 and the Motor Speedway is as popular as ever since its rebuilding in 1946. From 1931 to 1940, Stephen Hadfield had operated the Motor Speedboat track on this once water-filled circuit.
(Photo: Stephen Copnall)

In 1971, the author stands by the Waltzer, made by Jackson of Congleton, which itself heads the line of rides, with the Speedway, Bowl Slide and Fun House behind. On the right is the entrance to the Satellite.

(Photo: Stephen Copnall)

The Flying Saucers in 1971. This ride was a much more popular 'big wheel' than the 1938 'Eli Ferris Wheel', which had a ten-year post requistion run from 1944 to 1954. An identical wheel operated at the park from May 2005.

(Photo: Stephen Copnall)

the Motor Speedway to a smaller, but more contemporary, Europa Go-kart Track. In so doing, they created space for new rides such as the Paratrooper, which was a spectacular success. However, several of their plans for expansion were frustrated. Having had an application to expand onto the coach park turned down, the Fire Brigade prevented another Silcocks plan – to drain and fill in the boating lake. Silcocks already had a second Waltzer and operated the Whirl-a-Round and the Self Drive Cars on the southern side of the park.

1972: There are plenty of crowds on this Autumn Sunday. The subsequent loss of the Noah's Ark and the iconic Art Deco tower, greatly damaged the coherent look of Pleasureland, which dated from the 1930s.
(Photo: Stephen Copnall)

Looking up North Road. The Pleasureland Pavilion was sited on the left for a number of years. The Flying Saucers, the Haunted Swing and 1001 Mirrors, the Cyclone and Wild Cat complete the scene, after the destruction of the Noah's Ark in September 1977.

Every space was used to set up new devices by any operator who cared to pay the rent and the appearance of Pleasureland became cluttered and untidy. By this time, the council policy of no duplication of rides was no longer being enforced.

Money set aside by the council for a new Disney-style entrance was never put to that purpose. Nevertheless, the Clock Tower and Art Deco Entrances, which had given the park a feeling of coherence, were demolished in 1974, to be replaced by the aforementioned Sky Ride. In 1978, Silcocks introduced two new devices to the central area, the 'Alpine Glide' and the 'Ski-Jump', both fast continental roundabout rides with undulating track. For this, the Satellite had to be moved and the track of the Minitrain reduced in size. After the death of Leonard Thompson in 1976, his son, Geoffrey, took over the reins at Blackpool Pleasure Beach, but was also free to turn his attention to expanding the business in Southport. The Thompson family bought out the Helters operation on Pleasureland in which Blackpool was already a major shareholder.

At the end of the 1977 season, in September, a fire completely destroyed the Noah's Ark and Trip to the Moon. Although William Homer Strickland's Noah's Ark's disappearance was a grievous loss to the park, it provided the catalyst for a turning point development in Pleasureland's history; the construction for the 1978 season of a brand new Pinfari steel and aluminium coaster, the Wild Cat, which was erected on the vacant site. A new dark ride, 'Journey into Space', was constructed under and over the last stretch of the Cyclone, giving the coaster the added feature of a short tunnel.

In the winter of 1978/9, the Cyclone station was rebuilt and its cars repainted with stripes and waves, similar to those of the Blackpool coasters. Despite objections from some stall-holders and other operators, the entrance from Princes Park next to the Cyclone was sealed off, but a further entrance from the Marine Drive via a bridge was opened, which led straight into Helters Amusement Arcade. The River Caves was completely renovated and given a new entrance.

Maintenance on the River Caves in the late 1970s.
(Photo: Shelley Ward)

Where the Clock Tower once stood there are flagpoles in this shot from 1980. The Sky Ride aerial cableway travels across the central rides area. The Wild Cat sports a tower, centre right, reminiscent of Southport's Figure Eight of 1908–1936

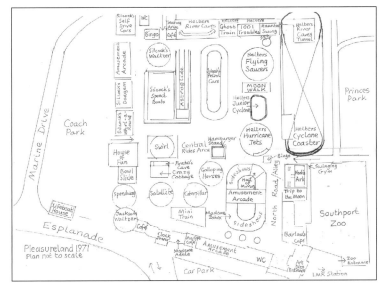

A plan of Pleasureland in 1971, showing the large collection of travelling rides that, at this point in the park's history, filled every available space.

(Photo: Stephen Copnall)

It was obvious that Silcocks and Helters, both rivals for the ultimate prize of Pleasureland, were now spending the money on investment that the council of whatever political complexion was unwilling or unable to spend. No solution using public money was in sight, as inflation soared. The 1979 'winter of discontent', and its political aftermath, would change Britain's industrial landscape forever. Only the resources of successful private enterprise would bring about Pleasureland's renaissance.

NINE

Blackpool takes the reins

A view across the Caterpillar to the Cyclone in the 1980s. Note the Paratrooper in full flight on the left, above the snack bar.

Leonard Thompson, Chairman and Managing Director of Blackpool Pleasure Beach for 47 years, had died in September 1976. After his death, his widow Doris Thompson became Chairman of the Company and his son, Geoffrey Thompson, became Managing Director. At a signing ceremony in the spring of 1982, Blackpool Pleasure Beach finally gained control of Pleasureland. Very soon, a different approach to the company's interests outside Blackpool would emerge after the aforementioned acquisition of the Helters operation in Southport in 1977, merging it with Hotchkiss Patents.

Sefton Council, who had taken over as landlords in 1974, were much more amenable and interested in private development. With effect from Good Friday 1982, a 60-year lease had been signed, giving Blackpool Pleasure Beach 65% of the concessions in Pleasureland, building up to total control in 2003, when the last of the leases of existing tenants would have expired.

Since 1978, Geoffrey Thompson had begun to develop an area at right angles to Pleasureland, running parallel with Marine Drive, known as Sportsland. Sportsland had started life as a slide park and then gained other novel attractions such as a Figure Eight Go-kart track, which opened in 1980. This park had replaced the sand hills, which had been popular with picnickers in the past. Gradually, the whole area up to the outer walls of the Sea Bathing Lake became a development area for Helters, as no space existed for new rides within Pleasureland. By 1983, a through way had been created under the Cyclone to the slide park, now known as Slippery Slopes, and beyond it a roller skating rink, a water chute style ride known as the Log Runner, a Mad Mouse wooden coaster, a Mississippi Steamboat, a Maze and an Alpine Chalet Café. This was an ambitious venture, which later gained the water slide from the Sea Bathing Lake, which was sold by the council to Pier Head Enterprises.

The Mayor of Sefton is watching a circus performance in the Pleasureland Pavilion in 1989. Mrs. Doris Thompson sits to the right, then Mrs Barbara Thompson and her husband, Geoffrey.

Geoffrey Thompson (left) riding around the new Go-Kart track which he had just opened.

From 1982 the **Log Runner** was a popular ride in the **Sportsland** area, now under the control of **Pleasureland.** Passengers were treated to two circuits of the track.

An aerial view showing **Sportsland** with its slides and **Go-Kart** tracks. In the centre, the **Southport zoo** is almost at its maximum extent. The **Looping Star** can be seen on the triangle near the curve of the **Kings Gardens.**

Loops of steel

Some things worked better than others, such as the Go-Karts and the Log Runner (an unusual combination of roller coaster and water chute). The Mad Mouse only lasted two seasons and may have fared much better had a site been found for it within Pleasureland. A similar problem existed for the sensational new ride erected in front of the main entrance on the Esplanade. This was the Looping Star steel coaster, which operated for three seasons from 1985 to the end of 1987, when the intention had been to move it inside the park.

The Southport Zoo, which had been extended to 4.75 acres along its northern side, was a well-established draw for those alighting from the Lakeside Miniature Railway and, in the 1980s, was marketed jointly with Pleasureland. The Zoo remained independent, but Sportsland was fully incorporated into Pleasureland which, as leases expired or were bought out, now took on more and more the appearance of a sister park to Blackpool Pleasure Beach. A book or sheet of discount tickets, giving access to all the rides operated by the new management, grew in importance year on year, pointing the way to eventual theme park status.

Until the mid 1970s, it had always been possible, outside business hours, to wander around Pleasureland unchallenged. Sadly, due to mindless vandalism, it was generally (and still is) necessary to secure attractions such as Pleasureland from marauding antisocial elements. Pleasureland was sealed off once the park closed to avoid any damage. Evening opening was increasingly focussed on special events such as firework displays, nightrider reduced price tickets and Halloween. A special newspaper advertising the events and new attractions of the

After the takeover of Pleasureland by Blackpool Pleasure Beach in 1982 some major rides quickly made their appearance. The Looping Star was one such ride, operating for three seasons between 1985 and 1987.

Pleasureland from the air in 1984. On the top left can be seen Sportsland, which had a new Go-Kart track. Sportsland was the only land at the time on which Pleasureland could expand. Behind the Cyclone is the zoo, which was acquired in 2003 for the purpose of further expansion.

In 1983 the Mississippi Steamboat and the Mad Mouse were erected on land adjoining the sea bathing lake and Marine Drive.

The River Caves by night in 1990.

season appeared once each year for free distribution. Pleasureland has remained a wholesome, happy place for families and people of all ages to visit.

Meanwhile, in the town centre, nightclubs, wine bars and restaurants were beginning to proliferate around the side streets behind Lord Street, which had itself become a very popular year round shopping destination for Merseyside and West Lancashire. In the 1990s, Liverpool and the Merseyside boroughs were able to profit from European funding initiatives, in particular Liverpool, which had been given Objective One Status by the European Union. This meant major investment in the city's future and, for Southport, many improvements to the town, such as help towards the building of Ocean Plaza and the new Marine Drive Promenade.

TEN

From now until when?

A view of the seashore Playground and Peter Pan's Pool in 1960, before a start had been made on the construction of the extension of Marine Drive, northwards. Alongside the pier the Lakeside Miniature Railway and station can be clearly seen. This whole area was devoted to children and included the famous Mary Willett Day Nursery.

(Photo: Southport Visiter)

The decade of the 1990s would see a seismic shift in Southport's fortunes. The first years of the decade – 1990 to 1994 – were a low point for the area around Pleasureland, but not for the amusement park itself, which was on the brink of a complete makeover. The need for stronger sea defences for Marine Drive, which had always been vulnerable to flooding, was becoming ever more apparent. The Sportsland part of Pleasureland had already reached the limit of its potential, unless and until Sefton Council embarked on its

The first drop on the Cyclone in 1996.

The Cyclone turnaround in 1991.

(Photo: Nick Laister)

By 1991 two dark rides occupied the northern corner of Pleasureland, the Ghost Train and Journey into Space. Already the children's rides have moved elsewhere in the park.

A 1992 view from the **Sky-Ride** showing the **Ski-Jump**, which operated for many years on this spot.

own projects for the area. This was, as always, a very slow process, reliant on government policies for the North West in general and on the chances of receiving European or National Lottery funding.

A dark shadow also hung over the council-owned Pier, now threatened with closure and demolition. The idea that this could even be contemplated was considered an outrage by most Southport citizens. Sandgrounders had already seen the total collapse of the enormous Winter Gardens shopping centre scheme in 1992, stretching out from Lord Street Bus Station to the Indoor Baths, so understandably believed that anything could happen. Construction of the Winter Gardens had reached the stage where the entire steel skeleton had been erected. If completed, the project would have brought thousands of shoppers straight to Pleasureland. How was it possible, after all the promises and pipedreams, for this scheme to fold? But fold it did, dealing a hefty blow to Southport's self-confidence.

Bye bye to bathing

Worse still, the Sea Bathing Lake, now in the hands of private enterprise, was closed and demolished in 1994, leaving the town without any open-air swimming facilities. The 'Pool', as the Sea Bathing Lake was known, had been the whole reason for the construction of the Marine Lake Bridge in the early thirties. The Colonnade at the entrance to the Marine Lake Bridge had been built as a concert party venue and then, in the 1950s, it became a successful roller skating rink. The bridge had given access to these magnificent corporation attractions, which sadly thus far have never been replaced. They also brought life and custom to other venues in Princes Park, when the area never had the empty feeling it sometimes has today. From the top of the chute in the Bathing Lake you could see the trains on the Cyclone at the highest point of the track. Princes Park now took on a deserted feel without the 'Pool' to draw the crowds both to it and ultimately to Pleasureland.

Happiland, the successor to Peter Pan's Pool and Playground, succumbed to a lingering death in the early 1990s, after struggling for many years in a neglected area of the foreshore. The Lakeside Miniature Railway now no longer had the profitable role of linking expanding Pleasureland with the once vibrant Peter Pan's. However, the one bright spot was the ongoing refurbishment of Southport's precious jewel, Lord Street.

Funding was finally obtained for the construction of the Marine Drive sea wall and new outer promenade. With its smart street furniture and attractive paving, the development was opened in stages from 1998 onwards. The effect was a total transformation deserving high praise for those in Sefton who had brought it about. Ocean Plaza, which went hand in hand with what has now become a major coastal traffic artery, reached a penultimate stage of completion in 2002. A new hotel, the Vue cinema complex, bowling alley, fitness club, retail park and skateboard facilities are, hopefully ,just the beginning, now that the magnificent suspension road bridge has been opened over the Marine Lake.

The Pier, after a successful campaign for donations from the townsfolk and those who loved

The Big Apple Coaster under construction.

**The Cyclone
station in 1993.**
(Photo: Nick Laister
Collection)

**Ocean Plaza
Retail Park where
Peter Pan's Pool
and Happiland
stood from 1930
until 1990.**
(Photo: Stephen
Copnall)

Southport from beyond, was eventually given lottery funding. Completely rebuilt, it reopened in 2002 and immediately became a huge success, being named 'Pier of the Year' in 2003. The Promenade Gardens were also renovated and replanted with high quality floral displays, although much remains to be done in other areas around and beyond the Marine Lake.

In Pleasureland, now renamed 'The Amusement Park on the Sands', the largest investment programme in its history had begun in 1998, culminating in the opening of the suspended looping coaster, the 'Traumatizer', in 1999. This had an electrifying effect on attendances which shot up to well over two million annual visitors, comparing favourably

The Skyride (seen here in 1996) affords us a wonderful view of the Mini Train, Caterpillar, Bowl Slide, Cyclone and Wild Cat.

In this picture, taken in 1999, marketing manager Steve Christian is surrounded by various suitably-clad men and women and raises a glass on the opening of the Casablanca Centre.

Steve Christian, Pleasureland's marketing manager, presides over the world record breakers for a backward-facing ride, the Cyclone.

with the much larger Blackpool Pleasure Beach, which boasts six million visitors each year. In the summer season the park in Southport remained open until 9pm and parts of Pleasureland, such as the new Casablanca Entertainment Centre (which opened in 1998) and the Fun House (refurbished and extended in 2000) were available to the public throughout the year. Gradually the season, in various guises, became one that lasted for all but the Christmas period and its January aftermath, a far cry from previous decades, under council control, when Pleasureland opened on Good Friday and closed entirely for the winter at the end of September.

Chaos and the death of the sideshow

Meanwhile, in 1997 the swing boat ride, 'Tidal Wave', made its appearance on North Road, drawing to a close a brief period when roundabout rides, such as the Alpine Glide and the Himalaya, came and went. The last remaining rides operated by other showmen were taken over by the Thompson management. The sideshows continued, but as their leases ran out they gradually disappeared from Pleasureland, until in 2003 all the tenants in this category left the site and the Thompson family finally had complete control.

In 1998, the 'Chaos', the first gravity ride of its kind in Europe, was opened on North Road. From 1999 onwards, a major investment programme each year enhanced Pleasureland's image. With full control of the park, the Thompson family could focus on improving the park's infrastructure as well as introducing exciting new rides. The Casablanca had replaced the site of cafes which went back to 1922. King Solomon's Mines was the name given in 2000

The Himalaya was a very popular ride in the 1990s, but very costly to operate. Behind is the Journey Into Space, which would later become the Ghost Train.

In 1985 Jan de Koning's Looping Star opened on the Esplanade car park in front of Pleasureland. At the end of the 1987 season it was moved elsewhere in the UK, as space could not be found for it in the park. This spectacular ride was the forerunner to the Traumatizer, erected in 1999.

(Photo: Paul Fourdrinier Photography, Southport)

Below: The King Solomon's Mines roller coaster under construction in 2000. This ride previously operated at Morecambe's Frontierland as the Wild Mouse and Runaway Mine Train. (Photo: Nick Laister)

In this shot from 2000 the large amusement arcade stands in the shadow of the Log Chute. The Millennium Wheel was at Pleasureland for the 2000 season only.

Geoffrey Thompson, seen here in 2000 at the opening of the wooden coaster, King Solomon's Mines. Hollyoaks stars Stephanie Waring and Keith Richmond are about to cut the ribbon.
(Photo: Peter Owen Creative Photography, Lytham St. Annes)

Hollyoaks starts Stephanie Waring and Keith Richmond in 2000, enjoying the opening ride on the popular wooden coaster, King Solomon's Mines.
(Photo: Peter Owen Creative Photography, Lytham St. Annes)

A tree planting ceremony in 2001. Geoffrey Thompson is holding the spade: he was responsible for the huge improvements in the appearance of Pleasureland. The occasion is the 25th anniversary of Geoffrey Thompson as MD of Blackpool Pleasure Beach Ltd and Mrs Doris Thompson as Chairman.

Left to right: Helen O'Neil PR consultant to Blackpool Pleasure Beach, Geoffrey Thompson, Pat Collier, personal assistant to Geoffrey Thompson, Steve Christian, marketing manager of Pleasureland, Phil Pickett, general manager, Stuart Cragg, personnel manager. Kneeling is Jim Goff, chief engineer.

to the completely rebuilt wild mouse type ride, a wooden coaster from Morecambe's Frontierland, where operations were being rationalised. The ride, sited between the Waterboggan and the Dodgems, was opened by Hollyoaks stars Stephanie Waring and Keith Richmond, in the presence of Geoffrey Thompson and his son Nick.

In 2001, at the same time as the refurbishment of the Fun House, a new Games Plaza was opened. The main event in 2002 was when Geoffrey Thompson invited celebrities Neil and

A view of Pleasureland taken from the Millennium Wheel in 2000, showing the new Traumatizer roller coaster, the Cyclone roller coaster and the new games area in the centre of the picture. Gradually the ramshackle sideshow booths would be replaced by these modern units. (Photo: Nick Laister)

The opening of the Lucozade Space Shot (2002). From left to right, Christine and Neil Hamilton with Geoffrey Thompson. (Photo: Peter Owen Creative Photography, Lytham St. Annes)

**The neat
sweep of the
Waterboggan
and the King
Solomon's Mines
frames the
entrance to the
Lost Dinosaurs
of the Sahara
in 2004.**
(Photo: Stephen
Copnall)

Christine Hamilton to open and ride on the Lucozade Space Shot, a 120 feet high shot and drop tower. This has proved not only to be a landmark ride, but also an extremely popular attraction to the teens and twenties.

In 2003, Geoffrey Thompson invited another celebrity, Jeremy Beadle, to open 'Abdullah's Dilemma', a revamp of the old Haunted Swing and 1001 Mirrors, now combined into one attraction. At the end of the season the entire acreage of Southport Zoo was purchased for park expansion, compensating for the loss of much of the southern flank of Pleasureland, when it had become a coach park in the remodelling of 1949. In the early summer of 2004, rebuilding of the River Caves into the 'Lost Dinosaurs of the Sahara', the extension of the 'Desert Rescue' children's ride and the opening of another gravity device, the 'Sandstorm' (formerly the Astro Swirl at Blackpool Pleasure Beach) on North Road, completed the scene.

All seemed set fair for Mr Thompson to realise his ambition, along with that of his father, Leonard Thompson, to make Pleasureland second only to his beloved Blackpool Pleasure Beach. He had achieved so much since taking on the long-term lease in 1982. Thanks to his business drive and care for the town, the acquisition of the zoo site would provide a major opportunity for further remodelling of the park and new rides. Tragically, on 12 June 2004, at the age of 67, Geoffrey Thompson died suddenly.

At the time of writing, Geoffrey Thompson's daughter, Amanda, has taken over the running of the Company. What the future might hold for Pleasureland is not known. Sefton Council's current plans for the seafront show that it intends to remodel and landscape this area as well as extending Ocean Plaza. Perhaps the Lakeside Miniature Railway, the Model Railway Village and the Marine Lake will not be forgotten in this scheme. Whatever the future brings, Southport has reason to be eternally grateful to the Thompson Family that the new theme park of Pleasureland is now the number one attraction in the town and one of Britain's most popular amusement parks.

ELEVEN

Southport's other attractions

Anglers take advantage in 1954 of a spring tide beneath the newly decked end of the pier. The silhouette of Pleasureland is clearly visible in the background. (Photo: Klaus Gloede, Berlin)

The Pier

Southport's amusements were not confined to Pleasureland alone. There was never a 'Golden Mile' in the town, but Nevill Street, Scarisbrick Avenue and Coronation Walk catered almost exclusively to the holiday trade, leading as they did from Lord Street to the Promenade. There was even a Louis Tussaud's Waxworks to draw the trippers. At the Pier Entrance, now occupied by Silcock's Amusement Centre, there had once stood the Pier Pavilion and, post World War II, the Casino Theatre. From 1945, the Pavilion had the dual

function of a dance hall, as well as hosting musical events and concert parties. In the last season before the outbreak of war in 1939, it housed a small funfair. A description of the site in trade newspaper World's Fair gives a flavour of the time, describing the opening of the Easter weekend:

"The old theatre on the pier, transformed into an amusement arcade, had plenty of patrons. Outside there is a motor speedway … the dodgems are very fast and create unlimited fun. Gypsy Smith is the resident character reader here. Professor Pearson was advertised for his high-dive in flames (at the end of the pier) … Electric trams were taking visitors down the pier and back. They are reserved for this journey only."

After 1923/24, steamers could no longer call at the landing stage, but fishing and yachting remained possible and popular to this day, at high tide. This part of the pier was badly damaged by fire in 1933, but the whole structure was acquired by the council in 1936. A new but slightly shorter tram service, with cars similar to the streamline ones in Blackpool, was introduced, there being an open boat car and a covered car with a centre entry and exit. The cars picked up the electric current from a third rail and the whole track ran on the south side of the pier deck. This replaced an older pier railway, which had gone as far as the pier entrance.

Shortly before the war, Southport Corporation began work on replacing the damaged outer end of the three quarter mile long pier. Concrete piles were already in place at the seaward end, ready for decking to begin, when the outbreak of hostilities put an end to any further work. The pier was closed to accommodate a searchlight station, in use during the air raids on Merseyside between 1940 and 1943.

Reopened after the war ended in 1945, Southport Pier had not been blown in two, as was the case with virtually every pier on the south coast, but the entire sands, north of Formby and Freshfield, were studded with anti-invasion posts. These were not removed until 1946. Always a major attraction due to its unusual length, the aim was to resume restoration work as soon as timber could be found. This was not possible until the start of the 1950s when, because of problems with the electrical supply, the tram service urgently needed replacing. The pier had a similar character to that in Southend-on-Sea; it was for walking and taking the sea air, rather than being a place of amusement, although it did sport the usual amenities such as a café and illuminations of a simple kind. In 1949, Southend Pier was equipped with a fleet of brand new trams, but in 1953 Southport opened a diesel powered miniature railway, built by Harry Barlow, who ran the Lakeside Miniature Railway. This was slower than the tram, but extended to a new station at the very entrance to the pier, where it had been up to the mid-thirties. At the same time the decking and renovation was completed at the seaward end, where an amusement arcade, a souvenir shop, a café and an open-air enclosure with seating and a stage for concerts, were provided. Another fire damaged the same area in 1959, and a larger café and sundeck were built on the site.

Eventually a replacement train for the pier railway was necessary before complete closure of the pier in 1996. The history of the pier has been fully covered in other publications, but today, thanks to generous donations and other funding which permitted complete reconstruction, a new era has dawned. Following its reopening in 2002, the emphasis is now on walking, recreation and education, although there is still an amusement arcade at the entrance to the pier. A new tramway is expected to be ready in the near future. For those who do not wish to ride to the end of the pier, admission is completely free and all of the structure is open to the public throughout the year. The response from residents and visitors alike has been overwhelming. A novel feature will be a tram stop at the Marine Drive, where there is already an exit to the beach.

Peter Pan's Pool and Playground

Peter Pan's Pool and Playground opened in 1930, on the site of Southport's first open air bathing pool. The construction in 1928 of a much grander Sea Bathing Lake had freed the area on the northwest corner of the Marine Drive, alongside the pier, for other development. As Pleasureland at the time was not over-endowed with children's rides, Maxwell, Manners and Pring, a company that had operated a boating lake and other amusements on

The original open air pool, to the north of the Pier, which would eventually become Peter Pan's Pool and Playground, two years after the opening of the Sea Bathing Lake. The crescents of changing cabins were retained as premises for cafes, shops and seating areas, when Maxwell, Manners and Pring took over the site to develop it as a charming children's amusement park.

Blackpool's North Shore from 1925, saw the potential, situated as it was on the sands near the seashore playground by the Marine Lake and Mary Willett's Day Nursery. The Pier Station of the Lakeside Miniature Railway was a mere hundred metres away.

Maxwell, Manners and Pring operated other sites in Brighton and Southend under the name of Peter Pan's Playground, but in Southport the word 'Pool' was added, as the water of the redundant open air baths was used for boating. A sandy enclosure for swings and slides was made with a separate small admission charge. A wooden track was built for petrol driven mini motor cars and several devices erected such as the 'Wendy Glide', a skooter-like car which a child could straddle as it ran downhill along a steel track. There was a chair-o-plane ride called the 'Dive Bombers', a 'Jungle Train' and a 'Jigsaw Railway', where tubs whirled at every twist and turn. Catering for large numbers of parties was another speciality of this delightful amusement park. There was also a real mascot St. Bernard dog called 'Nana', based on JM Barrie's book.

Although Sunday opening was not permitted (except for boating), due to Southport's Lord's Day Observance Society's powerful presence in the town, Peter Pan's Pool and Playground was largely unaffected by the war. Unlike the devastating blow dealt by requisition to Pleasureland, most of the rides at Peter Pan's continued to operate. It was therefore in a much healthier financial position in 1945 and ready to embark on a programme of expansion.

Harry Barlow extended his Lakeside Miniature Railway to a new station opposite the entrance to Peter Pan's in 1948, followed in 1949 by Maxwell, Manners and Pring's construction of a large paddling pool. More rides were added by the company, which also ran operations at the Casino up the road and the Motor Boats and Motor Speedway in Pleasureland. A new entrance was built to enhance the appeal of the park. Until 1960, business was brisk, but when the company was offered another long lease, a new trend had begun to manifest itself. Children were becoming more sophisticated and some families were starting to take package holidays in warmer climes. Eventually, Maxwell, Manners and Pring pulled out of Southport altogether.

By the early 1970s the name of the park, under different management, was changed to 'Happiland'. A valiant attempt was made to extend the choice of rides, by constructing a Dinosaur Ride on the sand hills opposite, adjoining the pier. Trampolines and other playground equipment were installed, but Pleasureland and the adjoining Sportsland, with its larger slides and Go-Karts, proved to be too great a counter-attraction.

Happiland was put up for sale after the close of the 1989 season. The specification was as follows:

"Developed as a Children's Amusement Park and separately fenced Playground together with an on-site car park which can accommodate four hundred plus cars. The rides include: Ghost Train, Viking Boats, Santa Fe Train, Jet Ride, Magic Roundabout, the Wheel and Giant Astroslide.

An advertising poster from 1965 describing Peter Pan's Pool and Playground in its heyday. As children became more sophisticated and Pleasureland expanded the number of rides on offer, so Peter Pan's and its successor, Happiland, increasingly struggled to attract enough visitors.

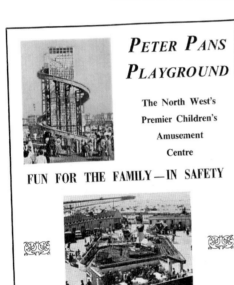

PETER PANS PLAYGROUND

The North West's Premier Children's Amusement Centre

FUN FOR THE FAMILY — IN SAFETY

PARTY CATERING IS OUR SPECIALITY

FREE BROCHURE AVAILABLE ON REQUEST.

FULLY OPEN EASTER TO OCTOBER.

View from the pier to Ocean Plaza and Pleasureland.
(Photo: Stephen Copnall)

"In addition there is a Gift Shop, a Snack Bar with patio, Ice Cream Kiosk and a large Arcade. Office Block and Café/Chip Shop. Toilets for Ladies and Gentlemen.

"The separate fenced Playground includes: An Entrance Kiosk Shop, Paddling Pool, Crooked House, Crazy Golf, Slides and Swings, Fun Castle, Trampoline, Deckchairs and Picnic Tables".

It is difficult to imagine how anything else could have been fitted into the grounds, but it was not enough to stop Happiland's decline and closure. The site is now submerged under a fast food outlet and car park, part of Ocean Plaza. Children are now catered for by a large selection of rides in Pleasureland, albeit different from those once operating at Peter Pan's Pool. A fitting epitaph to the lost innocence of a much loved place might be this description from the 1952 official holiday guide:

"On the other side of the Pier is the unique Peter Pan's Playground … a place designed for children only, with exciting roundabouts, motor-cars, aeroplanes, swings, slides and many other things to bring colour to their cheeks and a sparkle to their eyes. A fine boating lake and a lovely paddling pool have recently been added, just for the kiddies. Truly this is a wonderful Never-Never Land".

Lakeside Miniature Railway

The Lakeside Miniature Railway has always been an integral part of the attractions on offer to visitors to Southport. Opened as Llewellyn's Miniature Railway from White City to the Pier in 1911, it immediately became popular with its charming steam locomotives and green painted trains. Whereas many miniature railways were contained within an amusement park or had a circular track, the one in Southport served a real purpose, by linking the two destinations of Pleasureland and the Pier and later Peter Pan's Pool. It was extended in 1948. Passengers were offered single and return tickets and the line was busy enough to operate three trains on its 800-yard route.

In the inter-war years ownership passed to Mr Harry Barlow who built the Rowland Emett's Far Tottering and Oyster Creek Railway for the 1951 Festival Gardens in London's Battersea Park. During the 1980s, high tides flooded the Marine Drive station up to the first bridge. The construction of better sea defences did not come a moment too soon. When the previous owner of thirty years standing, John Spencer, sold the miniature railway for £225,000 to Don Clark and business partner Graham Leeming, the sale included four diesel electric engines, as well as the Red Dragon steam locomotive, which Mr Spencer had bought in the 1990s to carry on the tradition of steam hauled trains.

The Miniature Railway circa 1933, showing Pleasureland station. This attraction was very popular, remaining open throughout the 1939–45 war. The real steam locomotives and open carriages took visitors to and from the Pier station.
(Photo: Sefton Libraries Local History Unit, Southport)

The engine sheds of the Lakeside Miniature Railway.
(Photo: Stephen Copnall)

Already Mr. Clark has re-built the station entrance at the Ocean Plaza end of the line and he intends to re-build Pleasureland station for the 2005 season. To restore a balanced passenger demand, because there is no children's amusement park on the site of Peter Pan's, Mr Clark has plans to set up twenty trampolines and other equipment around the Marine Drive station to increase its potential as a visitor attraction. Also projected is a 'Thomas the Tank Engine' locomotive and train, which has great appeal to children and, as an idea, has been tried successfully on miniature and preserved railways elsewhere in the UK. There have been discussions with Sefton Council from time to time about a possible re-routing of the line in conjunction with the eventual redesigning and redevelopment of Princes Park. The Marine Lake is currently up for sale and there are no plans in the immediate future to alter the route of the LMR.

As Pleasureland expands onto the old zoo site, the LMR stands to benefit. If plans for the Aquadome Water Park at the other end of the line come to fruition, and the Marine Lake is revived as a major attraction, then this much loved railway, with its woods and waterside views, can indeed look forward to a rosy future.

Southport Zoo

For many decades in the Twentieth Century, there has been a zoo somewhere in Southport. Hesketh Park and the Botanic Gardens had aviaries and other attractions aimed at fostering a love of animals in children. The Zoo and Pleasure Gardens in Kew at the end of Scarisbrick New Road on the edge of Southport began life around the 1900s. It was reached by an electric tram route from the town centre and there was also a railway station for the zoo on the line to Altcar. However, during the 1920s the business folded.

The origins of the present zoo began in 1953 when Mr Frank Farrar developed one acre next to Pleasureland as a Pet's Corner. For the last 47 years, Doug and Carol Petrie ran the Southport Zoo and Conservation Trust on the same (but enlarged) site next to Pleasureland, taking over its management in November 1967.

A 1903 advertisement for Southport's first zoo on the eastern edge of the town.

A view of Soutport Zoo, with the Wild Cat roller coaster in action behind.

(Photo: Stephen Copnall)

The Land of the Little People, or Model Village, run by Merrivale Limited, was a beautifully landscaped oasis at the southern end of the promenade. (Photo: Stephen Copnall)

At the height of its popularity, there were over thirty different species of birds, animals and invertebrates. The animals lived in family groups and bred successfully. Within the zoo was a schoolroom and natural history museum, a picnic area with a playground for smaller children and a 'Pet's Corner Barn' for closer contact with furry animals. There was a reptile house and aquarium, a parrot house and primate house and even a hospital with an incubation room. An ideal family venue with a tea bar and gift shop, the Zoo was very popular for decades. However, as outright hostility in recent years has increased amongst certain pressure groups, the task of running an attraction next to an amusement park in a very public position, turned from one with obvious advantages in terms of attendance to one of being under siege.

Finally, with much regret, the Petries decided to leave Southport after having found good homes for the Zoo's occupants. The area will now be developed for new rides for Pleasureland.

Southport's Model Villages

The first model village in Southport came into being after the closure of the Cheshire Line's Committee Railway. The lines were generally little used and were closed at the beginning of 1952.

By 1954 Lord Street Station had been converted into a very useful 'Ribble Bus Station', and the area behind, up to the old bridge, from Rotten Row to the Promenade, became a development area for Southport's first model village. This was opened as 'The Land of the Little People' in 1956 by the Dobbins family, under the company name of Merrivale Southport. Thomas Dobbins had originally been an estate agent in Buckinghamshire, where they used

to place models of houses for sale in the shop windows. Close by was the Bekonscot Model Village, which already existed in the inter-war years, and was a major inspiration to him.

Thomas's brother Harry was given the task of running the Southport Model Village and another member of the family set one up in Great Yarmouth with the help of craftsmen from Southport. The gardens and models were of such a high standard that they could be compared with Madurodam in The Hague in Holland. It was a tragic loss to Southport that the business was bought out by speculative property developers for the ill-fated Winter Gardens shopping scheme in 1987.

Fortunately for Southport the torch was picked up by Ray and Jean Jones who were granted planning permission in 1994 to build a Model Railway Village in the South Marine Park near the Venetian Bridge. Construction began in 1995 and the attraction was opened in 1996 as a 15 year project. The Southport Model Railway Village has captured the magic of its predecessor and has become a very popular attraction with visitors to the town. The Model Railway Village has an educational purpose with questionnaires handed to visitors to complete. The working models, miniature trains and English villages in a beautifully landscaped setting are complemented by an attractive café and gift shop.

Palmists and Clairvoyants

An integral part of the traditional seaside holiday has been a visit to a clairvoyant and, until 2003, several palmists had worked on Pleasureland. Post-war as well as pre-war, this had featured as part of what was on offer amongst the many stalls and sideshows along the alleys and roads leading from the Clock Tower entrance. In the 1970s, Madame Adele and Madame Zohra read palms and gazed into the famous crystal ball. This work, as much in demand now as in the past, continues in Southport's Market Hall where Madame Irene works today, after more than 22 years in a booth next to the Sky Ride on Pleasureland.

1922–2004
Main Events relating to Pleasureland's Development

1922 Rides transferred from Southport White City to Pleasureland on new site at the behest of Southport Town Council's Improvement Committee. On 31 May 1922, WG Bean, Blackpool Councillor and Director of Blackpool Pleasure Beach attends opening ceremony with Southport Councillor Aveling and the Mayor and Corporation. Rides transferred from White City site include the Figure Eight Toboggan Railway, the River Caves, the House of Nonsense, the Cake Walk, the Helter-Skelter Lighthouse and Maxim's Captive Flying Machine. New rides include the Scenic Railway, the Bowl Slide, the Dodgems, the Whip and the Alpine Rapids Slide. Many sideshows and four cafes, painted in a uniform green and white colour scheme, laid out along railway sleeper paths occupy almost one half of the entire site. Some areas still await development.

1923 Southport Boating Company transfers its Water Chute from Marine Lake to a new site next to the River Caves. Alpine Rapids moves to another position on South Road.

1925 Mountain Caterpillar Railway opens within and alongside Scenic Railway.

1926 New Clock Tower Entrance.

1930 Noah's Ark opens.

1931 Ghost Train takes over Helter Skelter Lighthouse. Stephen Hadfield opens Motor Speedboat Track next to Water Chute Pond. In addition to Scenic Railway and Mountain Caterpillar, he operates the Dodgems, two roundabouts, a Cake Walk , the 'Scenic Studios' photo booth and an electric speedway, known as the 'Autodrome'.

1932 Pleasureland Illuminations begin in conjunction with 'Venetian Nights'.

1933 Last season of Maxim's Flying Machine to make way for start of council modernisation of Pleasureland.

1934 Art deco tower entrance opens fronting onto Princes Park.

1936 Last year of operation by Helters of their Figure Eight, Bowl Slide and Shooting Range to make way for Charles Paige to construct his Cyclone Coaster.

1937 Good Friday opening of Cyclone for Helters, now the number one attraction.

1938 Helters continue modernisation with introduction of Octopus and Eli Ferris Wheel.

1939 Leonard Thompson of Blackpool Pleasure Beach negotiates 30-year lease for the entirety of Pleasureland. Deal to be signed on 1/11/1939. Outbreak of Second World War forces postponement until cessation of hostilities.

1940 Pleasureland reopens in full under council control for summer season.

1940 Water Chute dismantled for scrap after Pleasureland closes indefinitely as hostilities engulf Merseyside. Water Chute Pond retained for future development at the request of Leonard Thompson.

1941 Requisitioning of Pleasureland by the Air Ministry put into immediate effect before the start of 1941 season. The Pier, many hotels and other buildings also requisitioned or closed. Peter Pan's Pool and Lakeside Miniature Railway allowed to continue operating. Blackpool Pleasure Beach open for business as usual, under certain wartime restrictions.

1941–44   Pleasureland sealed off to store aeroplane parts. Restricted area status. House of Nonsense destroyed by fire. Mountain Caterpillar dismantled /stored.

1944   Partial reopening of Pleasureland from July 1944 for rest of season. Most of park still closed to public with exception of Cyclone Coaster, Octopus, Noah's Ark, Ferris Wheel, some sideshows and a café. Access through Art Deco Tower only, as Clock Tower still in requisitioned area. Dive Bomber operating on site of former House of Nonsense.

1945   Reopening for full summer season, including Ghost Train, but two thirds of Pleasureland remain out of bounds, comprising the completely intact Scenic Railway and silted up River Caves, as well as many former sideshows and abandoned rides

1946   Scenic Railway sold to John Collins, the fairground operator, who rebuilds the attraction using the stored parts of the Mountain Caterpillar to make a Giant Big Dipper at Sutton Park to the north east of Birmingham. Pleasureland fully reopens after complete derequisitioning, but in a damaged and diminished state. The River Caves, the Motor Speedway in the drained former Motor Speedboat Track and the Water Chute Pond, now a Boating Lake for those displaced boats, make up the extent of the post-war grounds in proper use. Sideshows which have survived are all open. Negotiations resume with Blackpool Pleasure Beach. Stephen Hadfield's Autodrome operates in shadow of Clock Tower until remodelling of central area.

1947/48   Last two seasons in which Leonard Thompson tries to reach a satisfactory deal on the lines agreed in 1939. Negotiations break down resulting in continued council control. Southport's Borough Engineer instructed to draw up plans for modernisation and new layout of Pleasureland.

1949   Pleasureland opens in new guise. Colonnades on each side of Clock Tower replaced by walls, sleeper paths replaced with tarmac and large coach park, occupying a third of pre-war site. New central rides area includes a traditional caterpillar roundabout, a helter skelter, later to become a bowl slide, a leaning 'Crazy Cottage', 'Galloping Horses' and a waltzer. All sideshows rebuilt in a more compact area with a new amusement arcade. New house style of green and cream with red lettering.

1952   Hell Riders Wall of Death for one season only . Beginning of new line of rides to separate central rides area from coach park. Illumination of rides etc begins on modest scale. Wartime claims for compensation settled.

1953   Application for Fun House approved as well as moves to replace Dive Bomber with a Moon Rocket.

1954   Sunday opening of Pleasureland and other Southport attractions agreed. Children's Zoo opens next to Princes Park entrances.

1955   Moon Rocket replaces Dive Bomber.

1956   Famous Ducking Pond Bullseye sideshow ceases operation. Octopus is replaced by 'Hurricane Jets'.

1957   Roller Skating Rink opens.

1961   Cyclone badly damaged in January storm. Extensive rebuilding completed for beginning of season. 'Flying Saucers' big wheel opened by Helters in addition to the 1001 Mirrors and Haunted Swing, which are erected on the former site of the Dive Bomber/Moon Rocket.

1962–1969	More rides join central area including Mini-Train and Satellite.
1970	Silcock Brothers build multitrack Astroglide slide on part of Motor Boat Lake and Motor Speedway, which they are now running after departure of former operators from Peter Pan's Pool, Maxwell Manners and Pring.
1973	Further remodelling to make way for Silcock's 'Paratrooper', Europa Go-Kart Track and introduction of other devices, enlarging this operator's presence before the change of council from Southport to Sefton. A second waltzer from Silcocks duplicates that run at the other end of the grounds by Jacksons of Congleton.
1974	Council's plans to remove clock tower and art deco entrances and replace with one in the style of Disneyland fall through.
1974/75	Sunnysands Leisure erects aerial cableway, 'The Sky-Ride', after council demolition of both entrances. Sky-Ride becomes another major attraction.
1977	New Southport Indoor Swimming Baths open on Esplanade opposite Pleasureland, bringing more custom to the park. Cyclone completely refurbished as the enduring premier attraction. Disastrous fire in September completely destroys the Noah's Ark and Trip to the Moon. General malaise as foreign holidays, inflation and industrial unrest make their mark.
1978	Geoffrey Thompson of Blackpool Pleasure Beach takes over management of Helters Limited. New Pinfari coaster 'Wild Cat' opens as well as new dark ride under the Cyclone, 'Journey into Space'.
1980	Development of Sportsland. Opening of new Go-Kart Track.
1982	Blackpool Pleasure Beach Chairman and Director sign 60 year lease on Pleasureland.
1983	Tidal Wave swingboat ride opens as well as Mad Mouse and Log Runner on Sportsland, now part of Pleasureland.
1984	Fire damages Cyclone station, which is rebuilt immediately.
1985/1987	Looping Star roller coaster opens outside grounds fronting on Esplanade.
1991	Rainbow Ride and Chewits Log Chute open, the latter outside original grounds.
1993	Ski-jump operating.
1995	Last year of operation of Hurricane Jets.
1996	Himalaya ride opens on North Road.
1998	Oasis Café near former Clock Tower demolished to make way for Casablanca. Europe's first 'Chaos' ride opens.
1999	£5,000,000 Traumatizer opens.
2000	Giant Millennium Wheel operates for one season only on Esplanade site. Hollyoaks stars Stephanie Waring and James Richmond open wooden coaster King Solomon's Mines.
2002	Neil and Christine Hamilton open Lucozade Spaceshot.
2003	Last season of Jacksons of Congleton Waltzer. Jeremy Beadle opens Abdullah's Dilemma and Blackpool Pleasure Beach gains complete control of Pleasureland. Adjoining Zoo site acquired for major development.
2004	River Caves rebuilt as 'Lost Dinosaurs of the Sahara'. Desert Rescue children's ride extended. New gravity ride, the 'Sandstorm', opens. Pleasureland wins the 'Sefton In Bloom' award for its landscaping and floral displays.

Select Bibliography and Sources

'A Century of Fun' by Peter Bennett (Blackpool Pleasure Beach, 1996)
'A Survey of Seaside Miniature Railways' by DJ Croft (Oakwood Press, 1992)
'Roller Coasters, Their Amazing History' by Robert Preedy (Robert Preedy, 1992)
'Roller Coasters, Shake, Rattle and Roll' by Robert Preedy (Robert Preedy, 1996)
'Southport as it Was' by Joan Tarbuck (Hendon Publishing Company, 1972)

Other sources:
Blackpool Pleasure Beach and Pleasureland Archives
Cinammon Design, Hanover House, Liverpool, L1 3DZ
Paul Fourdrinier Photography, Southport
Peter Owen Creative Photography, Lytham St Annes, FY8 5HA
Peter Raymond Photography, Southport.
Sefton Libraries, Southport Local History Unit
Sefton Museums / Botanic Gardens Museum, Southport
Southport Official Holiday Guides
Stephenson's Guides to Southport / Southport Visiter Newspapers.
The National Piers Society
Photographic services to the Author, Annings Ilkley Limited.

All other sources are from the author's own archives.

May 2005 saw the opening of another Big Wheel at Pleasureland, run by concessionaire Richard Ryan. The Wheel, which previously operated at Southsea's Clarence Pier, is identical to the Flying Saucers wheel that operated at Pleasureland in the 1960s and 1970s.

(Photo: Richard Ryan)